BETWEEN THE LINES

BETWEEN THE LINES
Not-So-Tall Tales
from Ray "Scampy" Scapinello's
Four Decades in the NHL

Ray Scapinello and Rob Simpson

John Wiley & Sons Canada, Ltd.

National Library of Canada Cataloguing in Publication Data

Scapinello, Ray, 1946-
    Between the lines : not-so-tall tales from Ray "Scampy" Scapinello's four decades in the NHL / Ray Scapinello, Rob Simpson.

Includes index.
ISBN-13: 978-0-470-83834-1
ISBN-10: 0-470-83834-5

    1. Scapinello, Ray, 1946-. 2. Hockey referees—Biography. 3. National Hockey League—Biography.   4. Hockey—Canada—Biography. I. Simpson, Rob, 1964- II. Title.
GV848.5.S375A3 2006   796.962092   C2006-902233-X

Production Credits
Cover and interior text design: Michael Chan
Front cover photo: Dave Sandford/Getty Images
Back cover photo: Bruce Bennett/Getty Images
Printer: Friesens Printers Ltd.

John Wiley & Sons Canada, Ltd.
6045 Freemont Blvd.
Mississauga, Ontario
L5R 4J3

Printed in Canada

1 2 3 4 5 FP 10 09 08 07 06

To John Shannon, a man of his word
RSS

and to Maureen and Ryan, for all of their love and support
RAJS

Contents

Acknowledgments

Thank you to Scampy, Maureen, and Ryan, to the always honorable Dan Mathieson, and to Blake Corosky and Mike Harper (and JS Bidal, formerly) at True Gravity for making this publication possible.

Thank you to Karen Milner and her creative and talented cohorts at Wiley, including Liz McCurdy and Michelle Bullard.

For spinning yarns and/or otherwise adding contributions, thank you in no particular order to Leon Stickle, Paul Devorski, Mike Murphy, Stephen Walkom, Mark Pare, Wayne Bonney, Scott Driscoll, Brad Kovachik, Bill McCreary, Rob Shick, Wally Harris, Ron Foyt, Bryan Lewis, Scotty Morrison, Phil Shulman, Frank Henry, Bill Rowley, Matt Langen, Joe Bowen, Harry Neale, Terry Gregson, Dave Smith, Jim Gregory, Frank Brown, Gary Bettman, Clint Malarchuk, Scotty Bowman, and Steve Yzerman.

For information, facilities, and support, thank you to Benny Ercolani, John Halligan, Matt Loughran, and the gents at the Central Hockey League; to Bill and Mary Valpey for the "writer's pad;" to Nora for her unintentional reverse psychology; and to Ian for his understanding when Dad has to be away on "hockey business" and for the running hug when I'm finally home.

Oh yeah, and of course, thanks to Paul Tavares.

A sincere apology and a steak dinner to anyone deserving I may have omitted.

— RSS

Foreword BY SCOTTY BOWMAN

During a game in Buffalo, I was coaching the Sabres, and Scampy was on the lines. Early in the first period, Scampy blew his whistle and signaled an offside call as the opponent entered our zone. Scampy was moving to the face-off dot when I started yelling at him. "That was an offside goal! That was an offside goal!" I was ranting. I even stepped down over the bench, pushing two players out of the way, to get my foot on the boards in order to make myself more visible. Scampy thought I'd flipped my lid. He skated over and said something like, "What are you talking about, Scotty? It's a nothing-nothing game." I said, "In the game last week, that was an offside goal!" Now, part of this was because I actually thought Scampy had missed a call at one point in a game the week before, and I had a hard time letting it go. Also, I was simply giving him the business for no reason at all. We both found it somewhat entertaining. Ric Seiling, one of the players I pushed aside, reminded Scampy of this story a few years ago, and Scampy reminded me.

I'm usually pretty serious on the bench, as you know, but if there's one guy I didn't have a problem messing with just a little bit, it was Scampy. He had a great relationship with the players, the coaches, and everyone else at the rink. I could yell at him all night, but it wouldn't do any good for a couple reasons. First, I doubt he'd have a poor enough performance to warrant me yelling at him; and secondly, it wouldn't bother him if I yelled at him all night anyway. He'd let it roll off his back, and he'd do his job.

This is a guy who is very well-known for his profession-alism and his efficiency. If you talked to a hundred hockey people, I doubt one of them would have anything bad to say about Scampy. Even if he were to miss a close call, which I don't think he did very often, I doubt a player would say a word—they all have too much respect for him.

It was a pleasure to be included as part of this book about Scampy and his friends and life behind the scenes as an official. I had no idea about some of the different things he was up to off the ice, and it offers a fresh perspec-tive on a few of the NHL's most talked about games and incidents. It's also a testament to one of the more remark-able individuals ever to be involved in hockey. Scampy is truly one of a kind, and it was always a pleasure to have him involved in a game. He was around a lot, particularly the big games, and as you'll see, he earned the big games. He was working when we won it all in Pittsburgh and again when we had success in Detroit.

In December 2004, Scampy, a couple other officials, and I were on the same flight over to Moscow for Igor Larionov's farewell game. After we chatted for a while and I shared some stories and laughs, Scampy said to me, "Are you really Scotty Bowman?" I thought that was funny. Scampy shared that, over the years, he felt a little intimi-dated by me, by my record and success or whatever, and that he'd never even think about screwing around at all while I was on the bench. I think I surprised him with the fact that I was pretty talkative; I'm a lot friendlier off the bench. Whatever respect he had for me as a coach, I can say the feeling was mutual for him as an official. Scampy was a constant, a pro, a tip-top official for years and years, and when he was on the ice, I knew I had one less thing to worry about heading into a game.

—SCOTTY BOWMAN

Foreword BY STEVE YZERMAN

As I'm reading this book, looking back over Scampy's career, I'm thinking, wow; this guy's been on hand for most of our team's significant moments. He's been there for many, if not most, of my personal milestones as well. To think he's been around for my entire career, plus he started twelve years before me, and never missed a game, is pretty impressive. He lined the finals when we lost to New Jersey in 1995, and he lined the finals again when we won the Cup in 1997 and Detroit ended its long drought without one. He was there again the following year when we beat Washington. I didn't really think about it at the time because I was focused on the games, but Scampy was a constant through all of that, a familiar face, and obviously an excellent linesman: the World Cup in 1996; the 1998 Olympics in Nagano; and finally in December of 2004, when I played in Igor Larionov's farewell game, where Scampy was one of the invited on-ice officials.

Over the years, Scampy and I rarely had a disagreement. When we did, he was not afraid to speak his mind. Once we both cooled off, he would always come back with a light-hearted comment and a little smile just to ease the tension.

When I came back from an off-season knee surgery in February 2003, my first game was against L.A. When I went on the ice to take a face-off in the Kings' zone, Scampy was in the face-off circle and the crowd gave me a really nice welcome. Scampy stepped back from the circle and said, "Steve, let me know when you're ready." I had really hoped to quickly get back on the ice with as little fuss as possible, but I really appreciated Ray's consideration. I thought it was a very classy thing for him to do. After a moment, I nodded to Ray. He dropped the puck and the game resumed.

I found it interesting to read about Scampy's respect for Darren McCarty and a few of the other guys. I can honestly say the respect is mutual. I never realized Probert and Scampy swapped sweaters. That's the ultimate respect from a guy like Probie. Scampy has to know the fight game pretty well since he was always mixed up in the middle of it. To have the respect he does, and to control things as well as he has, is pretty amazing. He's not a big guy; I wouldn't be too fond of jumping into a melee involving Joey Kocur or Probert. Some of those guys around the League were animals, and Scampy jumped right into those battles for more than thirty years, without getting seriously hurt.

Throughout his career Ray conducted himself with the utmost professionalism and class. His calm demeanor, combined with an ability to react appropriately to any situation, are the reasons Scampy leaves the game with great respect and admiration from players and coaches throughout the NHL. He is a great man and a class act who will be greatly missed in the hockey world.

—STEVE YZERMAN

The Essential Scampy

Find a job you love and you'll never work a day in your life.
—Ray Scapinello, from Confucius

Klunk!

"Ouch! Damn! Ooooo …" And down goes Scampy.

With a month left in his thirty-three-year career, NHL linesman Ray "Scampy" Scapinello found himself bleeding profusely from above his left ear after getting beaned by a slap shot clearing attempt.

"It was more of a dull thud," Scampy points out.

It was March 4, 2004. The New York Islanders were visiting the Toronto Maple Leafs at the Air Canada Centre on a Thursday night. Scapinello was standing near the boards at the Toronto blue line. Shorthanded and unforechecked, New York winger Oleg Kvasha ripped the puck from his own blue line, right off Scampy's bald cranium.

"I stepped off the wall to give him the boards, and of course he had the whole middle," Scampy explains, "and instead he picks my head." Referee Bill McCreary stopped play. Off went Scampy to the training room holding a towel to the injury, only to return a few minutes later with seven stitches.

"Three doctors looked at me. One asked me where I was, while the other did the stitches. Another guy was looking at my teeth and mouth. About eight minutes later, the stitches were done and I returned to the ice just in time for a fight."

All this, not long after getting hammered by another clearing slapper right in the cheek of his buttocks.

"That thing was a big ugly bruise for weeks—a bruise on my ass the size of a dinner plate," Scampy declares.

Scampy had almost jinxed himself about three weeks earlier on a feature segment about him on Leafs TV in Toronto. At that point Scampy had never missed a regular season game due to injury, nor to anything else.

"I'm not sure why it hasn't happened … just lucky I guess," Scampy said on the TV show. This February 2004 statement qualified only as an "almost jinx" because just like the other times he'd been dinged up, Scampy finished the game. And of course, he was there for his next one, and his next one, and his next one, until his regular season career ended with game number 2,500 in Buffalo on Friday, April 2, 2004.

An inch in a different direction and Scamp could have lost part of his ear or been knocked out.

Maybe it was just dumb luck, or maybe, since he's only five foot seven and 163 pounds, some of the action went over his head—literally. "Luck" meant being built like a sturdy beer barrel, having evasive talents resembling Sonya Henie combinations, and a positive attitude that literally kept him in the game. Of course, another advantage was that as he lost his hair, Scampy became more aerodynamic.

"I think it's mostly preparation meeting dexterity meeting a sixth sense," explains Dave Smith. Smith, a former strength and conditioning coach for the New York Rangers and the Florida Panthers, was hired by the NHL in 1999 to monitor and improve the strength and conditioning of the officials. "I really believe Ray is a good genetic freak," Smith continues. "He kept a zest for the game when others may have burned out, he stayed in good shape and worked hard on it, and he was a good, strong skater. But more than anything, I think he was just built physically and mentally for the job. He knew what was going to happen before it happened and he was nimble enough to get out of the way."

Most officials will admit that it's impossible to duplicate Scampy's ability to be lucky, nimble, and clairvoyant. None seem to have his center of gravity or his sixth sense.

Brad Kovachik, who's been in the NHL as a linesman since 1996, missed a few games in early 2004. He was in San Jose at the Shark Tank when he got hammered by a dump in.

"All I remember is, it was one of the Sharks, I think a Russian guy," Brad explains. "He ripped it off the boards; it took a funny hop and smashed me right in the back of the jaw." Kovachik suffered a slight concussion and missed a couple of games. "I guess Scampy's record is safe from me," Kovachik adds.

Veteran linesman Mark Pare (pronounced Perry) came into the League in 1979 and won't be threatening perfect attendance either.

"I've been pretty lucky with injuries, nothing I'd consider too serious," Pare claims. "Some cuts and bruises from pucks." On Easter Sunday, April 16, 1995, Pare lost his front teeth. The Blues were hosting the Red Wings, while on a routine puck drop just inside the Blues' zone, St. Louis defenseman Steve Duchesne brought his stick up and hit Pare in the mouth.

"Duchesne was on my left," Pare explains, "the puck was cleared to our right, he turned and started up ice and lifted his stick into my mouth. Just a weird thing. I don't have any reason to believe he clipped me on purpose. Knocked out a tooth, a crown, and chipped a couple more. I spit them into my hand." Between periods Pare was stitched up, but it was days before he got dental work back home in Ontario.

Scampy still has all of his own teeth.

"I think through experience, I learned to read the play," Scampy points out. "It's not so much luck. I think eight times out of ten, if I read that the player with the puck was going to do one thing, he'd end up doing it. Based on where a player is on the ice, and where I was on the ice, I knew what they were going to do with the puck before *they* did." Scampy was blessed with this extra sense and developed it through experience.

Referees, meanwhile, tend to operate in a different area of the ice. They spend more time in the end zones in closer proximity to the puck carrier.

CHAPTER 1

"It doesn't matter if you're a ref or linesman," Scampy says, "you either read the play well or you don't. Sometimes it's simply unavoidable, but you shouldn't regularly be getting hit by the puck, whether you're operating along the neutral zone boards or in the corner."

Even the really good referees are not immune to the experience of pain, though. Unfortunately, the little orange band on their arms does not emit a force field. Paul Devorski has been beaned by pucks more times than he cares to remember.

"Never missed a game because of it," he points out, "but I did almost have my ear severed off once."

Devo, as Devorski is known, was working a game in Florida on February 15, 1999, when he nearly lost half an ear. It was late in the third period and he was backing up gradually along a corner as Dave Lowry of the Sharks rushed back into his zone to take out one of his former teammates. As the two players came together near the loose puck and Lowry finished the check, his stick whipped up and hit Devo in the head.

"Instead of slamming into the glass, his stick slammed me," Devo confirms. Play continued for another minute or so up and down the ice as Devorski repeatedly put his hand to his head to check the wound. Finally, after a whistle, with blood dripping from the side of his head, Devo skated over to the Panthers' trainer.

"Oooo, that looks pretty bad," the trainer pointed out.

"Listen," Devo said, "there's three minutes left. We can either hold this game up while I get stitched or we finish it." Devo decided to finish the last three minutes. For about five or six minutes of real time, he skated around with blood dripping down the side of his head.

"They wouldn't let me do that now—we throw players off the ice for bleeding. Things have changed quite a bit ... blood's considered dangerous," Devorski explains. Finally the game came to an end. "As I'm skating toward the gate to get medical attention, San Jose assistant coach Paul Baxter, a pretty tough guy in his day, says in a grumbly voice, 'That's a way to f——ing suck it up, Devo!'"

"Hey, I just want to get the hell out of here," Devo responded with an anguished smile. Without going into a training room, Devorski sprawled across two chairs in the tunnel with his head tilted up, and a doctor reconnected the two halves of his ear.

"No freezing spray or anything," Devo adds. "We didn't want to miss our beer." Seventeen stitches and off he went.

"Scampy was unbelievable, just unbelievable," he finishes, "to go as long as he did."

Devorski started as an official in the NHL in 1986. He, Pare, and Kovachik represent the norm. Injuries happen to everyone, and the older one gets, the more likely injury will occur. It's natural for a man's timing to slow down and his dexterity to fade. At least, it's natural for everyone not named Ray Scapinello.

In January of 2004, then NHL Director of Officiating Andy Van Hellemond described Scampy's longevity. "Ray's terrific conditioning and his ability to stay in great shape, and to perform into his late fifties is terrific, and it's a real credit to him that he's been able to do that. He worked hard at it; he's a Hall-of-Fame official for the NHL. His numbers are terrific, but just being a hardworking guy and a good representative of the NHL for thirty-three seasons is a real feather in his cap."

Port Alberni, British Columbia native Rob Shick ref'ed his first NHL game in April of 1986. He's worked a number of big nights with Scampy.

"Ray's the eighth wonder of the world," Shicker declares. "For so many years he did the same thing night after night—he didn't take nights off. And fifty-seven-year-old men just don't do that. He led us around the ice. It was actually good for the young kids and for me. We'd watch him go and think, well if he can do it ... "

Scampy's ability to stay injury-free is particularly marvelous to Shick, who's been injured on countless occasions. As one of the smaller referees, Shick's 160-pound frame has been bounced, pounded, and thrashed. About half of his injuries have been via the puck, and the other half from being run over.

"I've had six concussions, I think," Shick points out. "One of them came when I had five teeth knocked out at Madison Square Garden. I was cut with a stick while I was standing along the boards and I was spittin' 'em out like Chiclets. Thirty stitches. I wanted to go back out on the ice but I'd lost too much blood and plus I couldn't blow the whistle."

"Back in early 2003," Shick continues, "I was run over by Danny Markov in Phoenix. He just plowed me, and I had Jell-O legs. After I flew home the next day, I jumped in my truck to drive home and I had to pull over part of the way. I felt dizzy and I knew something was wrong and I just couldn't figure it out."

Shick was driving on the wrong side of the freeway.

"I couldn't remember my home phone number for a while. I had to write it down and carry it around with me," Shick adds.

These are obviously not good signs for his future considering Shick's track record of running into on-ice trouble. Apparently officials shouldn't be overlooked in the ongoing analysis of hockey injuries and concussions.

"We fall under the exact same umbrella as the players so that if we're hurt during a game, we're examined by the same dentist, or doctor, or orthopedist that the players are examined by," Scampy says. "For some of the more whiny officials, they call in the team pediatrician."

It's NHL policy that the home team training staff and doctors take care of injured officials just like they take care of injured players from either team. If any on-ice personnel suffer injury, the home team doctors take responsibility, all the way to the hospital.

And while on the subject, unfortunately for Rob Shick, there's more. "One night in Los Angeles, Shayne Corson skated over my arm. The muscle and tendon were hanging out ... "

Alright, alright—enough already about Shick and his injuries.

~

How's one "little" guy get so carved up in eighteen seasons while another can go thirty-three with nary a serious scratch? It's the aforementioned luck, conditioning, and sixth sense. Especially marvelous considering the fact that Scampy worked through what most observers would consider the NHL's goon years. Forget line brawls—in the 1970s, bench-clearing brawls were a common sight. There were bodies flying around, fighters falling, and Scampy right in the middle of it. In terms of injuries to officials, it's surprising that more linesmen are not injured breaking up combatants who seem to get larger and larger with every passing season.

"The brawls probably looked a lot worse than they actually were," Scampy declares. "I've been punched going in a bit early; maybe the other linesman didn't grab a hold of a guy. I've been punched a number of times, never enough to go down or anything. I've been pushed in the heat of the battle, where I've thrown players out for being over-aggressive. I've been pushed aside, bumped, and shoved. Through luck, or maybe because I have a thick head, I just managed to never get hurt."

Long-time linesman Leon Stickle survived those early melees as well, only to get squashed during a routine bout later in his career. A six foot two, 230-pounder, Stick started in the NHL in 1970, a year before Scampy, and he worked until 1997. His worst injury occurred in 1989.

"On Long Island, New Jersey's Jamie Huscroft and the Islanders' Mick Vukota were fighting," Stick begins. "They moved around a bit, some other players got close, a pile kind of developed and I was under it." The pile included six foot three, 210-pound Huscroft, six foot two, 225-pound Vukota, and Stickle. Stickle tore the anterior cruciate ligament in his right knee. He missed the rest of the 1988–89 season and much of the 1989–90 season. "This was before all that arthroscopic surgery," Stickle explains. "Pete Fowler out of London did a great job with my surgery. I think he used part of my patella tendon to help repair my ligament, but it was still a knife job back then and the recovery was brutal. The worst part was, it was my gas pedal foot ... I couldn't drive ... it drove me nuts!"

Scampy remembers countless times having skate blades whiz by his face as players fell down.

"Luck and positioning," Scampy declares.

Scott Driscoll wasn't so lucky. He missed some time on the ice after a fight-related injury. The Seaforth, Ontario, native joined the NHL linesman ranks in 1992. His injury in January of 2000 would make many folks squeamish. Not Driscoll.

"I was a biology major," he explains, "so when I got cut, I kind of liked looking at all of the stuff inside."

There must be bad mojo on Long Island, because like Stickle, Driscoll was also knocked out of the linesman line-up at Nassau Coliseum. Dave Scatchard of the Islanders squared off with Sandy McCarthy of the Flyers and they dropped the gloves.

"It was an emotional game, one of those rivalry games, both teams were fired up," Driscoll says. "I think Scatchard knew he was a bit outmatched, a big size difference, so when Sandy went to throw a punch, Scatchard ducked under and hip-threw him. Sandy went flailing down and his skate blade came up across my pants and jock and then across my right knuckle."

It took a moment for the players and Driscoll to realize what had happened. The blade had cut a slight, clean line through Driscoll's pants and across his jock area. It then cut a not-so-slight, real clean line through his hand. Scatchard, who had fallen to his knees, looked up at Driscoll and uttered, "Oooo."

McCarthy spun himself back in Scatchard's direction, looked up at Driscoll's hand and went, "Oooo." The two players stopped their scrap immediately and separated, while Driscoll skated over to the bench to have a trainer take a closer look at the deep, inch-long cut.

"I moved the skin around," Driscoll explains. "I could see the muscle and white tendon. It was actually pretty cool. I had studied anatomy." From a medical standpoint, Driscoll's luck matched his level of fascination. Of the rotating team doctors from the clinic the Islanders employed, the physician working that night happened to be a hand specialist.

"He sewed my finger back together. The weird thing was, I could still move my hand and fingers. It had cut right across my right ring knuckle. It was kind of numb," Driscoll remembers.

He missed the rest of that game of course, was fitted with a splint, and missed two more.

"I was home for a week," Driscoll recalls. "We had a kid nine months later."

So apparently injuries aren't a bad thing; they're a blessing.

～

Wally Harris was an NHL referee from 1963 to 1983 and despite at least three concussions, never missed a game in nineteen seasons.

"Guys played differently," Harris states of that time. "They never lambasted the puck out of the zone, they carried it. They played positionally. You knew where things were going."

"Yeah, high-off-the-glass [to clear the zone] became more prevalent as time went on," Scampy confirms. "But that's changed again. They're back to the eighties and nineties again this year [2005] with the new rules. One thing that helped us back in Wally's day was the rink was the same size but the guys were smaller, a little bit slower in general, and not as powerful. You can get crushed nowadays. They're bigger, stronger, and faster."

Harris was so confident in his feel for the game he actually officiated a few games with a broken shoulder. "I was doing a game in the American Hockey League in Providence. It was an odd rink," Harris remembers. "The bench gates opened onto the ice. Keke Mortson of the Hershey Bears swung the door open, I ran into it, tumbled into the dasher, and broke my collarbone. I spent New Year's Eve in a Providence hospital. Five days later I was back on the ice with my arm strapped down. There's no way you could do that now."

Harris spent some time in the AHL before moving up to the NHL permanently. These days, some lesser-experienced referees and linesmen will still occasionally go back and forth to the minors until permanently installed in the big league.

Besides the "lambasting of the puck out of the zone" nowadays, with the big bodies and two referees, there's simply more congestion. There's no question the game has changed a great deal since Wally was skating around with one functional arm.

Scampy managed to completely survive those early years and this present "big body-high traffic" era as well.

"That blew me away," an impressed Dave Smith declares. "When I heard he hadn't missed a game I found it incredible. I obviously knew from his conditioning what kind of shape he was in, but with all the travel and everything else, it just blew me apart."

Smith uses Ray as an example when he speaks about exercise and conditioning to other groups. At fifty-seven, Scampy's physical attributes are still strong, and many believe Ray could easily keep on working.

"Ray's just carved out of an old rock," Smith figures. "He was stubborn with work ethic, good nutrition, and he limited the beers. When guys get time off they knock off too many beers. Scampy was good with moderation and he wasn't a garbage eater."

When Smith began working with Scapinello in '99, Scampy was fifty-two years old.

"He wore a heart monitor," Smith continues, "let me run tests, and present new ideas."

For believers of mind over matter, Scampy as well supports that concept. He thinks "young" and never takes himself too seriously, even in the most important situations.

"It's a way to relieve pressure," Scampy points out. "It's common knowledge there's a lot of pressure calling games. I don't bottle it up. I like to have some fun, break the ice, and get guys ready that way. I knew what was at stake for the players and owners and such, but I wasn't going to sit around like a zombie. I was very comfortable in my environment, being ready and being loose."

It's this balance that has allowed him to be that lovable little bald guy, yet incredibly well respected at the same time.

Besides his regular season numbers, Scampy worked a record 426 playoff games and appeared in twenty Stanley Cup Finals. The Cup Finals number is the most astounding because getting to that point is completely subjective. NHL officiating supervisors monitor games and contribute reports from all around the League, and ultimately the Director of Officiating decides who goes to the playoffs and who moves on from round to round.

"If two guys are evenly matched in terms of performance, I'm sure a relationship here or there would put one guy over the top," Scampy assumes. It's not something anyone ever told Scampy to his face, but it's logical, and it's reality. "It's completely subjective. If you don't go on in the playoffs, you'll go to the boss and say, 'What's going on here?' 'We like your work, you're going along fine, but such and such is doing a little better. He's moving on.' You don't have a leg to stand on."

Scampy was considered the best in the business in 1980, 1981, 1983, 1984, 1985, 1986, 1988, 1989, 1990, 1991, 1992, 1993, 1994, 1995, 1996, 1997, 1998, 1999, 2000, and 2004. Was the boss playing favorites? Doubtful. During that time, four different men—Scotty Morrison, John McCauley, Bryan Lewis, and Andy Van Hellemond—ran the officiating department.

Being rewarded the ultimate assignments had nothing to do with the buddy system; it had everything to do with professionalism.

"Pride of workmanship," Scampy states. "Sometimes you think you should be working that big assignment and it hurts when you don't get it. Probably ten guys could go out and do a great job, but only four linesmen work the Stanley Cup Final series."

While Scampy is all-time number one for all officials, his friend from Guelph, Ontario, and twenty-year NHL veteran referee Bill McCreary is no slouch either, having ref'ed the third-most Finals games ever, behind only Bill Chadwick and Andy Van Hellemond.

"Ray and I have spent a lot of time together over the years," McCreary points out. "The biggest word for him is professionalism, on and off the ice. He treats every single game the same way. It's as much a pleasure working with him in October as it is in May. That's rubbed off on me—made me a better official, and a better person."

～

To Scampy, it's even more important to be consistent off the ice. He lives by the golden rule, treats others the way he'd like to be treated, and it's not uncommon for him to go out of his way.

Maple Leafs fan Matt Langen and his father showed up at least two hours early for the last NHL game ever at Maple Leaf Gardens on February 13, 1999. The two wanted to take in the atmosphere and pick up a souvenir or two. That's exactly what the elder Langen was doing when Matt ran into Ray and Maureen Scapinello in the ticket lobby. Matt stopped Ray to tell him how much he appreciated his efforts as a linesman and how much he enjoyed watching him work. Scampy was thrilled, and after chatting for a few minutes, he invited the twenty-four-year-old fan into the rink with him.

"Scampy told the security guys around the building I was his nephew," Langen says. "We went all over the building, the nooks and crannies, I met the other officials, I saw the dressing rooms. It was amazing." It was during this tour that Matt explained how he was lucky to be alive. At age seventeen, the former Mississauga bantam, drafted by Niagara Falls of the OHL, had been given a fifty-fifty chance to live a year, because of his battle with leukemia. By the time he met Ray, Matt had received a bone marrow transplant from a Richmond, Virginia, woman in 1993, and his disease was in remission.

"Things had started to turn around for me," Matt says, "and the day with Scampy was just the capper. It was special for me and my dad to share that day and that game, although I did leave him out in the lobby without a ticket for two hours. He was looking for me while carrying around a framed picture of the first and last game programs from the Gardens."

"What a great kid," Scampy says, "and a fighter. I mean, they had written him off when he was a teenager, said it would be a miracle if he lived, and there he was, better than ever."

Matt's story had been told in the *Toronto Star* newspaper, mainly because he was diagnosed the same year he was drafted into major junior hockey. Matt was in the hospital regularly from October 1992 to May 1993. Although he went through agonizing sessions of chemotherapy, was constantly ill and lost his hair, his passion for hockey and for the Maple Leafs grew unabated.

"I sent Ray a copy of that article, along with a golf shirt and a thank you note," Matt says. "We've stayed in touch. I've gone to games in Buffalo with him a couple of times. 'Wear a suit and come with me,' he says."

Scampy also helped Matt get a job in hockey. He forwarded Matt's résumé to the NHL Players' Association, where six months later Matt landed a job in the computer department in May of 2000.

"It's a lot of work, but I love it," Matt explains. "I work on the private site for the players, about seventy or eighty hours a week during summer salary arbitration time, and then update everything else on the site basically 24/7."

Matt says he'll stay in hockey, and doctors say he's cured of leukemia.

"They call it a cure," he says. "I go back once a year to make sure I'm still in full remission." Matt lives with his wife of three years and their two-year-old twin daughters in Georgetown. He and Scampy talk a couple times a year.

~

Scampy's respectful treatment of people from all walks of life, and his dedication to his work on the ice, are the two broad reasons why he's earned unparalleled respect from others.

Bryan Lewis started as an NHL referee in 1970, became a supervisor in 1986, and three years later became the League's Director of Officiating. As Scampy's boss, he never once reprimanded Scampy for a poor performance.

"Never," Lewis affirms, "and I don't recall him ever complaining about an assignment, even when we'd lean on him in a scheduling pinch. I'd always go to him if there was a last-minute need, injury replacement somewhere, or something, and he'd just say, 'I'll be there, boss.'"

At training camp, Lewis never had any advice, corrections, or directions for Scampy either, because Scamp always arrived prepared to give his best.

"The only analyses I'd ever give him, or the only report I'd write," Lewis says, "is I'd draw a picture of the top of his head. Once a year, I'd sit in the stands, look down at the top of his head and draw the picture, suggesting that maybe he should try wearing a helmet. That was it; that was my one simple message."

Lewis has worked with young up-and-comers in the Ontario Hockey Association, where dozens of NHL officials have developed, and he now works as an advisor to the ECHL.

"I tell a lot of Ray Scapinello stories," Lewis points out, "but the one I use most often relates to a linesman's guidance and assistance for a referee. I'll never forget, early in our careers, in Atlanta, a group of Flames players were all over me about a disputed goal. A melee was developing in the corner when Ray skated around behind me and firmly stated, 'Bryan, you have to count the goal.'"

It was pretty simple. Scampy had seen it go in; Lewis hadn't. The confident linesman emphatically supported his referee.

"I pointed to the net, blew my whistle, and away we went. That's the type of firm support a referee needs and desires. If I see a young linesman lacking in guidance and assistance, he gets a Ray Scapinello story."

~

When Frank Henry, the NHL security man who has worked in Buffalo the last eleven years, was contacted to contribute a story to this book, his conclusion was, "I'm honored that you'd even call me for a comment on Ray. He touched everyone, and they'd always come away with a smile."

Henry managed to return the favor. He helped put a smile on Scampy's face on the occasion of his final regular season game, April 2, 2004.

"It was about two months before the end of the season," Henry begins, "and Scampy and I showed up at the rink at about the same time. Scampy always seemed to be the first official there." Scampy would drive himself down from Toronto.

"Gee, Frank," Scampy said, "I want to talk to you about something."

"Yeah, Scamp," Henry replied.

"Well, very few people know this—I've kept it quiet—but this is going to be my last season," Scampy said.

Henry had mixed emotions.

"The fans really took to Scampy in Buffalo. They respected him, cheered for him. I don't know what it was," Henry explains. "I was happy he'd get to retire and be with his family, but I didn't like the fact that the end of his career was coming up."

"Well," Scampy continued, "I wanted this to be the place for my last game because it's where I started. I've got a lot of friends and family that I'd like to have come in. Now, I don't want any freebies or any special treatment, I'm just wondering if you could check with the guy who runs the box office, so I can buy fifty tickets for the last game of the season. Or if you could, get his card in case I need to call him."

"Sure, Ray, I'll talk to my contact down there. I'll see what we've got and I'll grab Mike's card and you can give him a call."

"Thank you, Frank, that's great," Scampy replied. "Here, take my credit card—"

"No, no, that's okay. Just wait. Let me check this out," Henry said.

So as Scampy went to prepare himself for the game, Henry went over to the box office to talk to Assistant Manager Mike Tout.

"Mike, Ray Scapinello's last game is here in Buffalo and he wants fifty tickets to the game," Henry explained.

"What's the date?" Mike asked.

Henry gave him the date, April 2nd against Toronto. After a very brief moment Mike went expressionless.

"Uh oh," he said. "That's Toronto. That game is sold out. I don't know how to get him any tickets for that game." At least half of the building would be full of Maple Leaf fans making the relatively short drive across the border. Even if Buffalo wasn't in the playoff chase, this game would be a sellout.

Stunned and worried, Henry walked back down by the Zamboni entrance just as Scampy and the other officials were walking to the ice. Scampy smiled and gave Henry a thumbs-up.

"How's it goin'?" Scampy asked as he walked by.

Henry mumbled, "Uh, fine, fine." Everyone went on about their business. Finally, at the end of the game, Henry made his way back near the officials' room.

"As they're coming off, I feel lousy," Henry says. "I gotta tell this guy I can't get tickets."

As he's standing there, Henry noticed Sabres General Partner Larry Quinn walking by. Henry and Quinn had known each other since the days in the War Memorial Auditorium. Quinn helped move the team to the new rink and he eventually helped with the process of getting the team sold to Thomas Golisano in 2003.

"Hi, Larry," Henry said.

"Hi, Frank, what's up?" Quinn answered.

"Ray Scapinello wants to have his last game here in Buffalo," Henry started.

"That's terrific," Quinn responded.

"Ahh, the only thing is, it's the Toronto game and he wants to buy fifty tickets. I spoke to Mike, and it's sold out."

Without much hesitation, Quinn responded again. "C'mon, take me into the room and introduce me to Ray." Quinn remembered in his late teens and as a young adult watching Scampy officiate games at the old auditorium. The two men entered the officials' room and Scapinello and Quinn were introduced.

"Frank says you want to do your last game in Buffalo," Quinn started.

"Yes, sir," Scampy answered.

"Well, Scamp," Henry stepped in, "the game is sold out."

Ray slumped his shoulders as the other officials looked on quietly.

"Well, Ray, don't worry about a thing," Quinn interjected. "We'll take care of it. You'll have fifty tickets for your friends and family," he concluded.

"Ahh, what do you want me to do, what—" Scampy was cut off.

"Nothing," Quinn finished. "It'll be taken care of." The officials were speechless. Quinn and Henry left the room.

"Oh my God, who was that guy?" Scampy asked his cohorts.

"How are you going to do it?" Henry asked the Sabres' boss.

"Don't worry, I'll do it, and as it gets closer, I'll let you coordinate it," Quinn answered.

A week before the event Henry asked Quinn about the arrangements for Scampy's last game.

"Mr. Golisano has decided to give Ray and his family the private club for that night. They're going to have a private meal; they'll eat, they'll drink, all they want," Quinn stated.

"What time can they arrive here?" Henry asked.

"Let's say two hours ahead if they want," Quinn responded.

Quinn expressed to Henry what Scampy had meant to the League, that he was a legend, and that the team, the fans, and the city of Buffalo wanted to show him some appreciation. The Sabres had actually called around and bought back fifty tickets from season ticket holders.

The night of the event, Scampy gave Henry a list of the friends and family he'd invited into the club. Security guards worked the two doors. Thirty friends were lined up until Quinn arrived and saw Scampy's wife, Maureen.

"Maureen, are these all of your friends and family?" Quinn asked.

"Yes," she said as she turned.

"Alright. C'mon folks. You don't have to wait here for a list, everyone can go right in. Follow us."

After a few minutes Henry asked Quinn, "How long after the game can they stay?"

"They can stay as long as they want."

"I can't say enough about what the guys in Buffalo did for my family," Scampy says humbly. "It was amazing. I can't thank them enough."

As it turned out, soon after Scampy had announced his retirement, his long time cohort and friend, referee Terry Gregson, revealed his last game would be that night in Buffalo as well. At some point, Scampy shortened his list, and gave fifteen or twenty of his tickets to Gregson's family and friends.

"I worked with Terry my whole career. This is Terry's night too," Scampy told Henry later that night.

NHL Commissioner Gary Bettman showed up for the send-off, as did "Uncle Jim," Senior Vice President of Hockey Operations Jim Gregory.

"Scampy calls me Uncle Jim," Gregory explains, "because it's a sign in his head that I'm the oldest bastard working." In reality, it's an endearing moniker of respect for the long-time, white-haired hockey executive.

"I was really taken aback that Mr. Bettman would charter a plane and show up for the function. That was a big surprise," Scampy says. Bettman stayed for the entire game and for the proceedings afterwards.

"I can't count how many times I watched Ray work," Bettman explained later, "and I can't count the number of times I saw this happen: Ray would make a tough call on an icing or an offside, and a player who disagreed with the whistle would throw his head back and get ready to argue the call—until he realized who had made it. You could almost hear the player think, 'Oh, it's Scampy.' So they never argued, because Ray was always hustling, always in position, and always honest. He treated every game like a big game, every play like a big play, and the utter respect he earned from the players, and all of us, was the highest possible compliment he, or any official, could be paid."

Fellow officials Bill McCreary and Brad Kovachik showed up. Kovachik requested the night off with the League so he could be there, and since he wasn't included in the fifty guests, he and his wife Natalie scraped up two tickets to take in the game.

Meanwhile, after years of enduring his practical jokes, Scampy's cohorts finally got a pretty good last laugh. During his final season, Scampy had been lobbying with everyone around the league for a Harley Davidson motorcycle as a retirement gift. He'd joke about it with anyone who'd listen. Kovachik remembers being with Scampy in Atlanta when the Maple Leafs were visiting.

"During a TV break," Kovachik explains, "we had to stand between the benches. Scampy goes over to Pat Quinn, leans in, and says, 'You know, Pat, I don't know if you've given it any thought at all but I'd really like a Harley motorcycle for retirement, and I was thinking, if you got every one of these players to donate a little money, that would be a nice gift for me, don't you think?'"

Quinn had a pretty good chuckle, and the players were laughing, too.

"Not many people could, or would even *try* to make Quinn laugh," Kovachik concludes, "It goes a long way— the comfort factor—and it goes along with the respect Scampy gets."

Paul Devorski concurs. "Pat Quinn would yell at everyone. He'd yell at Scampy, but at the end of the night, Scampy would have him laughing. He's the only guy who could get Pat Quinn constantly to laugh. Quinn isn't laughing very much at games."

So, the night of his retirement, a large Harley Davidson box along with a few other gifts sat hidden near the officials' room. When it came time for Scampy to lift the box, he found a wooden rocking horse and a tiny, six-inch tall Harley Davidson motorcycle.

"Those buggers," Scampy remembers.

The League gave Scampy a fancy watch and Gregory presented Scampy with a shadow box commemorating his first and last games in Buffalo. The line-up cards from the games were posted inside along with photographs. Thirty-three seasons after starting his career at the Auditorium, Scampy finished his run at the modern HSBC Arena, which had opened in 1996.

"I also gave him and Terry a brick from when the HSBC Arena was built," Henry adds, "and a net from one of the rink's original goals. I couldn't do enough for him and I can't say enough. Scampy was always a goodwill ambassador when he came to Buffalo, and I've never heard anyone say a bad thing about him."

Probably the evening's most poignant moment came when Henry escorted Scampy's son, Ryan, down to ice level before the end of the third period. When Scampy came off the ice, father and son embraced, Scampy gave his son his final linesman's sweater, and Ryan handed over one of his college jerseys.

Of course, Scampy's last game *wasn't* his last. He garnered yet another trip to the playoffs, had an exemplary first three rounds, and earned himself his twentieth Stanley Cup Final.

Big Games, Colossal Pressure

I had no idea the pressure you guys go through
in the Stanley Cup Finals.
—NHL linesman Wayne Bonney to his cohorts, after his
first Finals game, May 18, 1990

Ray Scapinello started officiating in the NHL in 1971. Eight seasons later, in the spring of 1980, he worked his first of twenty Stanley Cup Finals. Randy Mitton joined the NHL officiating ranks in 1972. Twenty-two years later, on May 31, 1994, at Madison Square Garden in New York City, Mitton was about to work his first-ever game in the Stanley Cup Finals.

"I think Randy was an excellent linesman," Scampy says. "But whatever goes into making that final decision, Randy never made it all the way through to the Finals. It's performance-based with a little politics and personality thrown in for good measure."

Mitton was nervous all day before the Game One match-up between the Vancouver Canucks and the New York Rangers, and why shouldn't he be? It was the biggest series, in the biggest town, in front of possibly hockey's biggest all-time audience.

At MSG, the officials usually have a small room just off the Zamboni tunnel, but for the finals, they had a much larger room right across the hall from the Rangers. The officials arrived a few minutes after 6:00 p.m. for the 8:10 p.m. start. Usually under such circumstances, they'd wander around for a little while, grab a coffee, and maybe sit in the stands for a few minutes. Mitton sat quietly in the dressing room.

"I wandered around a bit with Terry Gregson ... came back to our room to find Randy sitting there already half-dressed," Scampy remembers. "It was well before the time we'd normally get ready."

Mitton then finished organizing his gear and sat back down, ready to light a cigarette.

"Whoa, whoa, whoa," Scampy interjected. "This is strictly a non-smoking room!"

Mitton thought for a moment, held his lighter and dart aside, and said, "Well, I'll tell you what Ray ... either you let me have this cigarette or I'll take a heart attack."

After a good wide-eyed chuckle came, "Oh, okay, torch it up."

Mitton and Scapinello worked Games One, Three, and Five together, prior to Scampy working Game Seven with Kevin Collins, who had worked Games Two, Four, and Six with Gerard Gauthier.

The nervousness Mitton felt before the series was normal. Like a goalie not wanting to give up a soft goal in a big game, a linesman does not want to blow an offside call that leads to a goal. Not only would it be excruciating at the time, but the official's name would go down in hockey history, especially if the call determined the Stanley Cup presentation.

In 1994, with a huge TV audience ready to watch the Cup Final in New York, Commissioner Gary Bettman popped into the officials' room before Game Seven. This was not standard operating procedure.

"Are you guys nervous?" he asked.

"Oh, I don't know," Scampy replied sarcastically. "We just put the [cribbage] board away." Bettman snickered, not knowing whether Scampy was serious or not.

Of the many memorable moments in that Game Seven, a few of the most intense involved the linesmen near the end of the game. Ramping up to the close finish, Vancouver trailed 3–1 heading into the third period. Trevor Linden scored a power play goal at the 4:50 mark to get within one. The Rangers managed to kill off a penalty midway through the third, and were hanging on for dear life the rest of the way. With time winding down in the final minute, New York repeatedly iced the puck, resulting in three crucial face-offs in their own end.

"Those were ballsy icing calls by Kevin," Scampy points out, "really good calls." The Garden crowd didn't agree. One of the dump-outs barely made it the length, and some say Vancouver could have played it.

"One definitely could have gone either way," Scampy admits, "but Kevin put the onus on the team that shot it down. The Rangers were puckering, trying to end the game, and kept clearing the puck. He had to make the calls; a couple were too close *not* to call."

It's a double-edged sword: Had Collins waved any of them off, and had the game ended before it did, they'd still be talking about it in Vancouver. Canucks fans would have thrown out the conspiracy theory: Bettman wanted big market, center-of-the-media-universe New York to win. As Scampy pointed out, Collins put the onus on the Rangers, preventing a premature finish, and preventing those unfairness theories from ever being generated.

Meanwhile, Scampy was responsible for dropping the puck all three times in the Rangers' zone.

"The last one, with a couple seconds left, was probably the least fair face-off I've ever worked," Scampy recalls. "There was no way I was going to stop the mugging and cheating and movement going on for that thing. We'd have been there all night."

"Don't make me throw one of you guys out of this!" Scampy remembers yelling.

The League hierarchy brought the footage of that puck drop up to the officials' training camp the next year and included it in the video package. Just like the NHL players, all of the officials and their supervisors attend a camp in early September each year, but instead of 3-on-2s and power plays, they work on positioning, face-off procedures, and reviewing new rules. Each day for a week, there's classroom training, on-ice training, and conditioning classes. During the face-off segment of the 1994 camp, the linesmen reviewed Scampy's final face-off from three months before.

Someone said, "Boy was that a brutal face-off." Guys were spun around. Sticks were in the air. This was obviously not the ideal arrangement. Players are supposed to be onside, lined up across from one another; the wings are not supposed to be inside the circle; and the players are absolutely not supposed to tie each other up before the puck is dropped.

"What Ray did here, that's not what we're looking for …," Scampy mocks himself in third person with a laugh.

"The puck hit flat. The Rangers obviously weren't angry about it, and Trevor Linden didn't chase me down," Scampy points out. "I was mostly worried about a flat drop. It was crazy; it felt like an earthquake there was so much noise."

The Rangers hadn't won a Stanley Cup in fifty-four years. The fans were ready to blow the roof off the arena. Scampy was the lone figure standing between one final puck drop and the end of the game. He waited for the centers to square up, and he dropped the puck.

∽

Two weeks earlier, Scampy was on the ice when the Rangers eliminated the Devils in overtime of Game Seven of the conference finals. The winning goal will forever be remembered by the famous call made on TV in New York by Howie Rose, "Matteau, Matteau, Matteau … !" That was the wild moment for the fans. The wild moment for the officials came when New Jersey tied the game with less than ten seconds remaining in regulation. Off a Scampy puck drop in the Rangers' zone, the puck was sent on net and a scramble ensued. There was essentially a pile-up in front, and with a few seconds left the puck was jammed in. New York goalie Mike Richter went berserk, and charged into referee Bill McCreary along the end boards and knocked him pretty good. McCreary kept his cool and allowed Richter to stay in the game—a staunch effort in the face of bedlam. Of course, had he tossed Richter, he might never have escaped New York.

Eight years earlier, Scapinello was the focus of Manhattan ire. The Canadiens and Rangers were tied at a game apiece in the conference finals. In Game Three in New York, the Blueshirts were dominating, but Habs goalie Patrick Roy stood on his head and forced overtime. In the extra session, more of the same, with the Rangers controlling the shots and chances and Roy turning them away. After withstanding another New York onslaught, the Canadiens finally cleared the zone, and lightning struck.

Rangers' defenseman James Patrick stood at the left point, watching the play on the opposite boards. His partner, Willie Huber at the right point, tried to keep the puck in but it hopped over his stick. A mad dash ensued from both sides of the ice, and linesman Scapinello found himself in a perilous spot.

"I was on the blue line on the side with the benches, along the boards behind Patrick, and as the puck went back to the point on the penalty box side of the ice, it hopped the point man's stick," Scampy explains. "Seeing it hop the stick, Claude Lemieux got a head start and headed for the puck. Patrick, instead of turning towards open ice, towards the penalty box side where everybody's going, he turns the other way, toward the boards, and stumbles over me. Lemieux goes in, scores, game over."

It's a general consensus that neither Patrick nor lumbering Willie Huber on the other point would have caught Lemieux. Tell that to the New York fans.

"Don Cherry was the only guy who defended me," Scampy says, then paraphrasing Cherry. "What the hell is Patrick doing turning to the bench side when the play is on the penalty box side? What are you blaming Scapinello for? [Patrick] never would have caught him. Can't he turn to his right?!"

It's one of the few times Scampy ever remembers Cherry sticking up for the officials.

Treatment from the New York media was a different story. The incident was shown on the local news for a day and a half. Sportscasters put a little white box around Scampy, highlighting his position on the ice while describing the lowlight. It was an ugly time.

With this in mind, you'd think Scampy might create a low profile for himself during the day off between games. Nothing doing.

"The next day we went to the Meadowlands Racetrack over in Jersey and somebody who runs the track asked us to present the trophy for one of the races," Scampy remembers. "Me and John McCauley were down in the winners' area when they announced the presentation."

The fans heard Scampy's name and the whole place started booing. A bunch of people started running down to the fence along the track, near where Scampy stood. They gave it to him, called him every name in the book, and threw programs at him.

"Holy shit, let's get *out* of here," Scampy said.

The next night, Scampy worked with Kerry Fraser, and Fraser, who usually leads the way out of the officials' room, wouldn't go out on the ice first. This was his fun way to bust Scampy's balls.

"C'mon Kerry," Scamp pleaded.

"No, you go first," the ref replied.

As soon as Scampy hit the ice the fans started booing.

"I'm skating around and they're booing the piss out of me," Scampy smiles. "Pierre Larouche skated up behind me, whacked me on the ass and said, 'Don't worry about it Scampy, he wouldn't have caught him in a million years.'"

Unfortunately for Scampy, that wasn't the issue. He felt like hell because a player had tripped over him and it may have affected the game's outcome. Despite it being a fluke, and the fact that Scampy was exactly where he was supposed to be, the hubbub over the incident was tough to handle.

"That night on the news, they put the white ball on me, like the highlight ball. 'What's he doing out there?' they asked. It was ridiculous and somewhat humiliating," Scampy recalls. The incident stuck in his mind and nagged him for years. It stuck with the New York fans for a while too, because the Habs never looked back and went on to win the series in five games. Scampy did not like being the center of attention for something considered so negative by so many. For a linesman, the "any publicity is good publicity" theory definitely does not apply. The ideal scenario for an official is to go unnoticed and to not intentionally or unintentionally affect the results.

Coincidentally, fear of screwing up is part of the core mental preparation for an official.

"You know everybody's watching, you mess up, and when you come home the next day, you know you're gonna hear about it," Scampy explains. "I fear screwing up; it's one of my motivators. A psychologist may think that's not positive, a lot of negative thoughts, but that's the way it is."

Officials are driven to avoid things like the Patrick collision, whether it is an actual mistake, a fluke, or whether it is their fault or not. If the official is in the right position, ninety-nine times out of a hundred, nothing unfortunate or controversial will occur.

Fans see the game a lot differently than linesmen, especially as it relates to the big plays and big moments. A fan sees a great play and reacts; the linesman has already reacted, by doing his job as the play developed. If Alexander Ovechkin streaks down the wing, crosses the blue line, and rips one over Andrew Raycroft's shoulder for a goal, the Washington fans would go crazy with joy. The linesman doesn't care; his job ended when Ovechkin crossed the blue line on-side. Linesmen rarely remember who scores or who pulls off something amazing, because it's not their job to pay attention. Officials need to be myopic, watching the lines, the ice, the puck. They can't remember historical moments because they themselves are subtle elements of those moments. To be remembered for being a part of a big moment is bad.

Leon Stickle's big, bad moment came in Game Six of the 1980 Stanley Cup Finals when the Islanders won their first of four straight Cups, although Stickle's mistake wasn't quite as monumental as many casual fans are led to believe. Many believe Stickle blew an offside call on the Cup-winning goal by Bob Nystrom in overtime, when in fact, the blown call came earlier in the game. A big mistake, yes, on the Islanders second goal, but it wasn't *the* goal, *that* being Nystrom's. Of course, unfortunately for Stickle, the call did affect the outcome of the game.

"Mel Bridgeman and Clark Gillies were tied up skating along the boards. It had been a physical game, so I'm watching them out of the corner of my eye as they cross into the Philly zone," Stickle explains. "The puck went in, came back out, but when I saw it—after being distracted by the bodies in front of me—it was on the line via Butch Goring, and I waved it good. Goring fired a pass across to Sutter, who I think rang it in off the post. I mean, when you screw up, everything goes wrong."

The Islanders took a 2–1 lead on the goal at 14:08 of the first period. Philly actually came back to tie it 2–2, fell behind 4–2, then tied it again before losing in overtime. For quite a while, among Flyers fans, Stickle's name was associated with New York's win.

"Oh, I was very well welcomed, the next time I was in Philly," Stickle laughs, "even though it wasn't until the following December. They had banners. People were screaming at me. I mean, they're great fans, they're very into it, and they were letting me know. The best part, as I'm skating around, the fans are doing the 'wave' in sync with me, as they're booing. Great fans. They don't forget."

As it relates to putting up with grief in general, as part of the profession, Stickle sums it up best: "I never had a chance to screw up in a building that didn't have anyone in it."

~

In the perfect world, a linesman's big moment comes when he's chosen to do a game, well before the action starts.

Scampy explains, "The big moment comes days before the game itself: recognition, followed by the earning of an assignment based on that recognition. Game Seven or gold medal, you can sit down during the day and realize you're considered one of the two best linesmen in the NHL or world. You know the importance of the game, what's at stake, but our big moment happens beforehand.

"Then there's the anticipation," Scampy continues. "It's always great to be first on the ice, and when you take the ice for a Game Seven you're thinking many things. One is a proud thought—the players, the viewers of TV, and the fans in the stands see you skate out and they're thinking, 'Look who's working this game. These guys must be good at what they do.'"

In 1990, linesman Wayne Bonney worked his first Stanley Cup Final game. He worked with Ron Finn, Edmonton versus Boston, Game Two. After the game in the officials' room he expressed how incredible the pressure was, and how hyped he was the whole night.

"As I look back at it now," Bonney says, "that feeling hasn't changed. I could talk about it all day, but you'll never know how it feels until you go through it. It's unreal."

Stickle, who worked twenty-seven years in the NHL, doesn't so much remember the action of his first Final, but he does remember the aftermath.

"Montreal beat Boston in overtime to win the Cup," Stickle recalls. "I remember standing on the ice and watching the Cup being presented. That was neat. Working Canada Cups were a big honor as well," Stickle adds.

Referee Paul Devorski had a truly unique experience. After having worked three consecutive Cup Finals in 2001, 2002, and 2003, Devo worked the World Cup Final in September 2004 with his little brother, linesman Greg Devorski.

"That was pretty cool," the veteran ref states. "In Toronto, Canada versus Finland, our wives came down; our families came in for it. That was special. Hopefully Greg can get to a Cup Final and I can get back to one, and we can work together for one of those." (Partial dream come true: Both worked the 2006 Stanley Cup Final, but they alternated games and didn't actually work on-ice together.)

Devo missed a chance at four consecutive Finals in the summer of '04 because of injury.

"I had neck surgery," Devo says. "It was degenerative; I had bulging discs, probably from playing football and hockey as a kid. The pain got so bad during the Toronto/Philly series; I couldn't go on. The problem had been there for a while and it finally caught up with me." It was the only time the forty-six-year-old had missed action, or potential action, because of injury.

Paul is eleven years older than his brother. When Greg first entered the NHL in 1995, the two worked together often, the first time during Greg's first month.

"We actually worked our first game together in Detroit, against Winnipeg. Our parents and a couple of our brothers and sisters came down from Guelph," Devo remembers. "*Hockey Night in Canada* did a feature on us, showed our parents, showed us talking in the room before the game, Greg giving me the business. The other thing I remember was the other linesman, Bob Hodges. As a senior linesman, he helped out Greg a lot early in his career."

Unfortunately, as it relates to big game pressure and nerves, there is no instruction booklet, and the experience factor cannot be handed down.

The elder Devo's first Final was Colorado and New Jersey.

"For the first five minutes of the first game you're just floating around out there, and the place is just rocking. You're like a fan, a bystander, going, 'This is pretty cool.' Joe Sakic makes a pass ... hey, that's a nice pass ... then you realize, 'Hey, you better get your ass in this game here.'"

Like a skater's first hit, or a goalie's first save, a referee doesn't really settle in until he makes his first call, or is forced to take control of a situation.

"You put a lot of pressure on yourself, really pump yourself up," Devo explains. "You're a little more prepared for it the second or third time, but you're just as jacked. You're not really that nervous, you're just more aware, hyped. If you miss a trip during the regular season, you're pissed—*Shit. I missed it*—but you move on. In the Finals, you miss a trip, you might affect the Cup. Oh, shit, you don't want that."

Every post season official agrees: Think too much, and you're in trouble.

"It's definitely a job where if you're thinking about your peers watching, or where you have to go on the ice, then you might run into trouble," Devorski continues. "Block it out, react, don't think about anything."

"I'm more nervous leading up to the game," Scampy adds. "Even if I'm not leaving the house until 5:00 for a 7:30 game in Toronto on Saturday night, I'm thinking about the game at the noon hour. Once I get in the dressing room, those thoughts are generally no longer going through my mind, and when the puck drops they're absolutely gone. Then we just react."

With eleven consecutive Finals under his belt, Bill McCreary is halfway to being the Scampy of refs, and he's learned to handle every playoff game the same.

"You learn to treat it like it's any other game," McCreary says.

⤳

Of course, there *are* exceptions. In 1998, Scapinello and McCreary were part of a series of games that *weren't* like any other, at least for NHL officials. The officials were members of the first NHL crew ever to work in the Olympics, which went hand in hand with the first-time participation of active NHL players in the Games.

The NHLPA (Players' Association), the NHLOA (Officials' Association), and the IIHF (International Ice Hockey Federation) agreed that if the best players in the world were to be present, then a few of the best professional officials should be in attendance as well.

Once chosen, the officials' gig began with IIHF rules meetings prior to going to Nagano. The crew included linesmen Scapinello, Gord Broseker, Gerard Gautier, and Kevin Collins, and referees McCreary, Mark Faucette, and Kerry Fraser. The rest of the officials were amateurs from across Asia and Europe.

Scampy remembers that the first issue that arose was the mandatory use of helmets by officials.

"Three of us won't require helmets," Scampy remembers saying.

"That's fine gentlemen, then you won't be working the Olympic Games," the answer came back.

"I'm a medium," Scampy replied.

And the helmets came with visors, which became, particularly for a person as conspicuous as Scampy, a form of international hockey camouflage. During one game involving the United States, they were well into the second period when Scampy had to drop the puck in the left corner face-off circle. U.S. defenseman Chris Chelios kept creeping in, forcing Scampy's cohort to blow the whistle.

"Could you back up, please," Scampy turned and asked. Chelios snuck in again, forcing another delay.

"Back up!" Scampy scolded.

Chelios leaned in, squinted, and said, "Scampy, is that you?"

"Yeah, now back up!"

No name on the back of the jersey and a helmet for the first time ... somehow out of sight, out of mind.

The other early dilemma for the NHLers was the process of learning the international rulebook. There were different rules and different punitive measures.

"The stuff we'd call a minor penalty for in the NHL, some of it, in the Olympics, the guy would be ejected for. We were a bit panic-stricken over learning all the new stuff," Scampy says. "We didn't know any of the extra rules."

They had the thirteen-hour flight from Vancouver to Narita Airport to cram.

"We're gonna screw this up royally," McCreary said while studying hastily. Of course, the boys from the NHL did just fine, which was a mighty relief for NHL Director of Officiating Bryan Lewis, who ran into some early prejudice in Nagano. International sentiment among the IIHF muckety-muck seemed to lean toward sticking with amateur officials from around the world. There was a feeling that the NHLers would come in with a high falutin, holier-than-thou, big-time attitude. Understandably, the flak came from people who had worked four years to get to the Olympics, only to be nudged aside by the NHL presence.

"We, as a group of officials, didn't feel too good about that," Scampy thinks back. "My understanding was René Fasel, the IIHF head, thought we were just going to show up and be the cock-of-the-walk, and walk around like we owned the place."

Apparently, Mr. Fasel had forgotten about the humility of the officials.

"It was a massive thrill to be chosen to do those games, to be the first professionals involved," Scampy points out. "I'm not sure how he got the impression we weren't going to be effective and into it. It was the Olympic Games—we were extremely proud to be there."

Of course, as it played out, the NHL officials gave Lewis reason to be proud of their performance, professionalism, and demeanor, in an environment where international coaches and managers had a loud voice in deciding which officials worked which games.

"I remember Brian saying that when he submitted the names to do the games, the coaches and management were more than happy with the selections. That was nice, especially for the referees. Nobody said they didn't want to see this guy or that guy. That was a real tribute to those guys," Scampy says.

In the end, Scampy worked the gold medal game with McCreary and a Swedish linesman, and Fasel ended up telling Lewis how impressed he was with the NHL officials.

Most of the games, Scampy worked with a very efficient Russian linesman named Sasha. And first name is as far as they got in terms of learning the respective languages. They couldn't understand a lick, instead relying entirely on the non-verbal, international language of hockey.

According to McCreary, Scampy's hockey intuitions and knowledge showed itself even before the games began.

"We're flying over, Ray, Gerry Gautier, and myself, and it's a heck of a flight from Vancouver," McCreary confirms. "We chatted a lot, tried to keep busy, and of course Ray's fidgety. He doesn't really sleep." That's when McCreary popped the question.

"Who's gonna win these Olympics, Ray?" he asked.

"I think the Czech Republic," Scampy answered after a quick thought, "because of Dominic Hasek." He was right on.

Scampy and McCreary actually began their Olympic odyssey together in Toronto. They flew Air Canada to Vancouver, where they met Gautier, who had flown in from Montreal. With almost five hours of travel down, about three times that amount remained.

After crossing the Pacific Ocean and the International Date Line, they arrived two days later at Narita Airport, well outside of Tokyo. (This is always freaky for trans-Pacific travelers, especially for first-timers. If a passenger leaves Vancouver at 6:00 p.m. on a Wednesday, he arrives in Tokyo at about 1:00 a.m. Friday. Thursday never happens. The opposite phenomenon occurs on the way back, when a passenger will spend an entire Wednesday morning and afternoon in Tokyo, and then experience most of Wednesday again, upon landing in North America.)

"I might have slept an hour or so on the long trip. We had breakfast, lunch, dinner, and breakfast again," Scampy remembers.

When the officials arrived, their Olympic credentials were waiting for them in a secured room at the airport. The Olympic security man was emphatic about one thing: "Lose your wallet, lose your passport, lose your wife, but whatever you do, DO NOT lose these credentials."

After twenty hours of airports and planes, Scampy and the boys took a train to Tokyo, a little over an hour's ride, and then transferred to a bullet train, the Shinkansen, for the 120-mile ride northwest to Nagano. One form of transportation after another after another.

"I was lost," Scampy says. And needless to say, exhausted. "I don't sleep very well, if at all, on planes and trains." On top of it, their baggage was thrown on separate buses at Narita and arrived in Nagano a day later, following security inspections.

"I'll never forget my room in Nagano," Scampy says. "Obviously, I'm not a big guy by any stretch of the imagination, but I could almost reach across and touch the walls on either side." Finally, a society where Scapinello was physically just like everyone else ... only thicker.

Adding to the atmosphere was the aroma of sweet potatoes, 24/7. A local man had a stand selling the tubers outside the officials' door, with the same classical Japanese tune playing on his little sound box the entire time.

Pling, PLING, Pling, Pling-Pling-PLINGGGG ... Pling, PLING PLINGGGGG, pling-pling-pling-pling-PLING.

"He drove me nuts for twelve days."

The Olympics were a couple of days underway before

the officials arrived, about two days before the hockey action began. This gave the fellas a chance to take in a little culture. The officials visited a Shinto temple, where outside, smoke cascaded from a large incense burner. The plumes were meant to bring good health, so a couple of the guys tried to cure injuries by dangling their elbows over the smoke, or by waving it toward their backs. Scampy tried to cup some onto his head to grow hair.

"It didn't work," he laughs.

"What a bunch of hooey," someone else said.

"We also went up to see the sacred snow monkeys," Scampy remembers. "We trudged through knee-deep snow to see these snow monkeys. No disrespect, but these were silly monkeys."

The monkeys sat and lounged near a hot spring that was surrounded by snow. Tourists and locals alike were instructed by the monkey-keeper not to make eye contact with the monkeys under any circumstances.

"You weren't supposed to stare at them or they'd get their noses out of joint," Scampy says.

Pedestrians had to walk across a bridge to get close to their primate cousins and to check out the related monkey shrine, while many of the monkeys sat on the bridge staring out over the spring.

"After checking out the shrine, we're walking over the bridge, coming back, and a monkey is sitting there on the rail, facing out looking at whatever. He's got his back to me and Gordie Broseker. For some unknown reason, don't ask me why, Gordie hoofs the lower rail right below the monkey's ass," Scampy explains.

The monkey spun around and took a swing at Broseker, Gordie jumped out of his skin, and the two men were off the bridge like a shot.

"You stupid bastard," Scampy said. Needless to say, the two never messed again with the sacred monkeys.

"Gordie almost created an international incident, eh?" Scampy finishes. "I don't know what inspired him to do that."

The day-to-day cultural adjustments were just as challenging. The refs and linesmen stayed at a hotel, not in an Olympic village of any sort. Every day, the hotel laid out on the ground floor a buffet for its North American visitors, with selections including eggs, bacon, and pastries. The cooks were not proficient at cooking western-style food, and the language barrier made it difficult to correct problems or to make special orders.

"The eggs were runny and the bacon was raw as hell," Scampy recalls. By day three, the NHLers were in the kitchen helping to prepare breakfast. Scampy was the short-order cook, running the place.

"We learned four or five words. We had them giggling constantly, and it was a lot of fun." This was unusual, because in Japan, formalities rule the day.

"One other thing they did there that was interesting was when they cleaned the room, every door was left wide open. If you're at a hotel in the U.S. or something, there's no way you're leaving your door open, allowing people to walk in and out," Scampy says.

In Nagano, there was no chance of anybody stealing anything. Also, unlike North America, it's not standard procedure after eating at a restaurant to leave a gratuity.

"There, if you left a $5 bill on the table as a tip," Scampy continues, "the next day you'd go in there and it would be taped to the cash resister as lost money. They just don't give out gratuities."

As for the hockey action, as is the case with most big games or events, the officials don't remember a whole lot.

"The only game that really sticks out in my mind was Czech Republic against Russia and I don't even remember who won," Scampy says. He's not referring to the final, when the Czechs took the gold medal 1–0 against Russia; he's referring to the preliminary round finale played between the same two teams.

In a game marked by fabulous goaltending, Russia beat the Czechs in a thriller 2–1, when Valeri Bure and Alexei Zhamnov scored ten seconds apart early in the third period. It earned the Russians a quarterfinal spot against Belarus, while the Czechs were forced to play the United States. Of course, despite the harder path, Hasek led his team through Team USA, then, of course, Canada in a shoot-out, and then on to gold, and revenge, against the Russians.

"One nice thing, if anyone was screaming at us, or complaining, we wouldn't understand what most of them were yelling," Scampy adds.

Cooler heads prevailed throughout the Games on and off the ice, and they had to, since security, particularly around the officials, was extensive.

And while 1998 was pre-September 2001, the Japanese still had the sarin gas attacks in the Tokyo subway from March 1995 in the back of their minds. The dressing rooms were very much off-limits, even to NHL operations boss Brian Burke.

Unfortunately for Scampy and the boys, their Olympic hockey credentials didn't get them into other events like figure skating or bobsledding. They only saw hockey games.

"I went to the women's gold medal game, and boy, what a good hockey game. I was really impressed," says Scampy. "They were banging and crashing."

The female officials stayed at the same hotel as the men. Scampy congratulated them on a fine effort, especially impressed with one gal who was a police officer from Montreal. The male officials swapped sweaters and some equipment with their counterparts from other nations.

"One Russian guy was really good at mooching equipment," Scampy points out. "I gave that bugger all of my equipment—helmet, visor, shin pads, elbow pads, pants, and my whistle."

As the Games wore on, Scampy began to get a little homesick. The dining experiences, featuring menus with photographs of the food and names written in staggered English, were getting old. Here or there, he'd find an odd lasagna or spaghetti, but it paled in comparison to the Italian home cookin' available in Guelph. Meanwhile, watching TV while dining or in the hotel room meant one thing and one thing only: CNN International.

"It was driving me nuts," Scampy asserts.

After the gold medal game, the officials managed to find their way onto a bus with NHL bigwigs that was going directly to Narita. Burke arranged it, and it saved taking the train to Tokyo and then transferring for another ride out to the airport. The guys stayed at a beautiful hotel near Narita for a few hours, which was a greatly appreciated capper to their long stay. In the wee hours of the morning, they headed off to the airport for their flights, where the lines to check in were unspeakably long.

"As excited as I was about going and being part of it, and doing the gold medal game," Scampy concludes, "I was really happy when we landed in Vancouver and then Toronto. I was really happy to get home."

As for Olympic pressure, Scampy says he didn't feel that much in the gold medal game.

"Maybe it was because it was Russia and the Czechs and I wasn't familiar with all the players, and maybe it was because we were in Japan, so far away," Scampy recalls, "but there was more pressure in that New York final, tenfold."

It's all perspective. Referee Paul Devorski, who worked the gold medal game in Torino, Italy, between Finland and Sweden in 2006, sums it up a different way.

"I was scared shitless," Devo says.

CHAPTER 2

Two years prior to Scampy's Olympic adventure, he experienced the ultimate in *on*-ice international intensity. In fact, Game Three of the 1996 World Cup final in Montreal between the U.S. and Canada was the most intense game Scampy ever officiated.

Canada won Game One earlier in the week 4–3 on a Steve Yzerman overtime winner, followed a couple of days later by a ferocious victory by the U.S. 5–2. It set up a border war, on Saturday night, in Quebec.

"Oh, boy," Scampy starts. "If you forced me to pick the toughest game I ever did, that was it. It was mayhem."

At one point, during a commercial break, Scampy skated over to referee Terry Gregson to confer, or, regroup in this case.

"Terry, we've lost control of this game," Scampy nudged.

"What do you think we should do?" Gregson replied.

"I don't know, I'm just telling you we've lost control."

The game was continuously vicious. The battle for international bragging rights, at least between the U.S. and Canada, had never reached these heights. The best players from the two countries had never faced off in the Olympics up to that point, the U.S. was rarely a factor in a Canada Cup (the World Cup precursor), and hockey's popularity on a world stage and throughout North America was at an all-time high.

"I remember calling a major penalty on Keith Tkachuk for cross-checking a guy in the neck." Scampy continues,

"I mean, that never happens; for me to call a major penalty it has to be very serious. I saw it, Terry didn't see it, and I had to call it. He really crossed the line."

Prior to the start of the contest, the officials, with Gord Broseker being the third man on the crew, were well aware of the impact, the importance, and the expected intensity.

"We were nervous as hell. You try not to show it but you know what's at stake, and you don't want to screw up. You can't think about it but you do," Scampy says. It was dead quiet as the three men sat in their dressing room watching the clock tick down to the start of the game.

Bryan Lewis broke the silence by walking in.

"Are you ready?" Lewis asked as he looked around at the threesome.

"I won't even respond to that question," Scampy answered.

One of the three hot seats had actually changed prior to Game Three. It was a rare instance where an official had been taken off a game. Kevin Collins was supposed to be the second linesman, but one of the GMs or team officials had insisted on a change. Collins may have missed an off-side call that led to a goal in Game Two. Broseker was his replacement.

The high-flying intensity continued. Eric Lindros tied the game 1–1 late in the second on Canada's twenty-second shot on goal that period, before Adam Foote put the red and white ahead 12:50 into the third. Brett Hull tied it for the U.S. at 16:52 before Tony Amonte scored the game winner forty-three seconds later. Empty-netters wrapped it up, and U.S. goaltender Mike Richter earned the well-deserved tournament MVP.

~

It wasn't the first time a goalkeeper stole the show against the Canadians, or Canadiens. One of referee Wally Harris's fondest memories came on New Year's Eve 1975, when the world's foremost hockey clubs, the Montreal Canadiens and the Russian Central Red Army team, squared off in Montreal as part of what was dubbed the "Super Series." Two Russian teams, Central Army and Wings-of-the-Soviet would each play four games against different NHL teams. Although not an all-star match-up, the Russian teams were bolstered by players from the Moscow Spartak and Moscow Dynamo clubs. The NHL clubs went 2–5–1, with the lone tie coming in the premier match-up, Canadiens versus Red Army.

"The two teams just played hockey, and it was beautiful," Harris remembers. "I may have always been a little sadistic—I usually enjoyed the fights, the rough games, but this was just amazing hockey."

It was impossible not to admire Russian goalkeeper Vladislav Tretiak. He faced thirty-eight shots and was spectacular, while his stand-up counterpart at the other end, Ken Dryden, faced thirteen. The game ended 3–3. Claude Bechard and Ron Finn were the linesmen.

~

Of course, the "huge factor" changes from official to official, relative to experience, and even geography. A first playoff game in Detroit may be a big deal for a guy who grew up in Ann Arbor, where to a guy from Thunder Bay, it's no big deal.

Brad Kovachik loved the Bruins growing up. During a playoff game in Boston in 2004 against the Canadiens, his mind drifted back to those fantastic post-season matches against Montreal he watched as a kid in the seventies.

"Just to be a part of this is amazing," Kovachik said after the series. "I wouldn't have imagined this ten years ago, and this is my fifth year in the playoffs. I definitely have an appreciation."

Naturally, Kovachik's goal is to reach the Stanley Cup Finals. Thus far, he's been as far as round two, meaning a round three game will mean a lot more to him than it would to someone who's already been there.

"I heard the hardest thing is not getting there, it's staying there. Ray's record speaks for itself. It's astonishing. He's an incredible role model, a leader, and a really good teacher," Kovachik adds.

～

Often, officials will unexpectedly find themselves involved in games of huge local importance due to record-setting moments or simply for nostalgic reasons.

Goaltender Ed Giacomin spent ten seasons with the New York Rangers from 1965 through the 1974–75 season. After starting his eleventh year 0–3–1, the Rangers waived him. On Halloween of 1975, the Detroit Red Wings claimed Giacomin, and two nights later they played New York at Madison Square Garden. The quick turn of events gave Rangers fans a great opportunity to show management, and Eddie, how much they loved and appreciated him. Sentimentality oozed from the building, as the Rangers all-time wins leader started against his former club. Giacomin had tears in his eyes much of the evening, and at one point, he stood outside his crease, leaned on his stick, and wept, as the fans continuously chanted his name, "Eddie, Eddie, Eddie ..." following a long initial standing ovation. The chants echoed again and again, every time he touched the puck.

"The hair was standing up on my arms," Scampy remembers. "Although I'm focused on the job, between whistles and such it was tough not getting goose pimples. What an emotional time for him, that was really something." Rangers fans cheered for the Red Wings that night, and the visitors prevailed 6–4.

Twenty-seven seasons later, different rink, similar emotion. In February of 2003, Detroit captain Steve Yzerman returned from a prolonged absence following reconstructive knee surgery, this after stumbling and battling his way through the 2002 playoffs on the bad wheel, leading the Red Wings to their third Cup in six seasons. His return came with Detroit hosting the Kings, and when Yzerman came out for his first shift, the fans in the Joe Louis Arena went absolutely crazy.

"They gave Stevie an extensive, loud ovation as he came in to take the face-off," Scampy remembers.

At first, Scampy was about to drop the puck, but then decided to let the crowd and Yzerman have their moment or two. Instead of blowing the whistle, he backed up and said, "Steve, lemme know when you're ready and I'll come back in." The other Wings appreciated it, and the Kings didn't seem to mind a bit.

Scampy's decision made a big impression on the network television commentators handling the game, as John Davidson sang his praises.

"Boy, what a classy move by Scampy," J.D. said excitedly over the noise. "That's a wonderful gesture by a veteran linesman."

Yzerman waited, the crowd noise peaked, and he acknowledged them. Not one to milk it, in fact, more than likely embarrassed by it, Yzerman then quickly leaned in and said, "Okay, Scamp."

"I blew the whistle and dropped the puck," Scampy says. "That was one of those things that came naturally to me, and came with experience. I guess J.D. really sang my praises. I'm not sure I deserved that, but I guess not everyone would have thought to have done it. It was a huge distraction and a big moment for Yzerman."

Fortuitous scheduling led to a nifty double-whammy for Scampy in Pittsburgh; he worked Mario Lemieux's retirement game in 1997, and then three-and-a-half years later in late December 2000, he worked the game against Toronto in which Mario returned to the line-up.

"At the end of his retirement game, still wearing my skates, I made a point of rushing around to where he came off, to shake hands with him, congratulate him, and wish him well," Scampy recalls.

He also recalls the incredible outpouring of emotion when Lemieux returned.

"He scored less than a minute into the game, I remember that," Scampy says. Pittsburgh beat the Leafs 5–0. "I was just lucky to be there, one of those things."

~

For younger officials, luck meant getting Scampy as a lining partner.

Scott Driscoll ponders, "I worked almost all of the big games in my career with Ray. My first playoff game was with him on April 16, 1997, Phoenix at Anaheim. I really remember that because Scampy bought me lunch that day, although the only reason he did it was because he knew I'd be buying the [playoff] rookie meal after the game," Driscoll adds with a laugh.

Driscoll's first Game Seven was also with Scapinello, in the 2001 Eastern Conference Semifinals between Pittsburgh and Buffalo, which went to overtime.

"The added pressure is fun, and we thrive on it. It was great working with Ray, especially because he gave me so much confidence," Driscoll points out. "He taught me a lot of things over my career, but he'd never overwhelm you with new information. He'd feed you a little bit here and there and let you work with it."

"A lot of the stuff is off-ice," Driscoll continues. "When I came into the League, I came from a small town of about 2,000 people. I didn't stay in New York City the first four years because I was a bit intimidated; I'd stay outside of town or on the Island. Lo and behold, you get familiar … cabs, subway, it becomes second nature. Once you've conquered a lot of that off-ice stuff, it makes the job a lot easier."

Driscoll's first conference final Game Seven was with Ray as well, as was his first Cup Finals, both in 2004.

"As a kid, I also worked a lot with Ron Asselstine, Bob Hodges, and Leon Stickle," Driscoll points out, "pretty solid veterans to learn from, but again Ray taught me the most, because he was always there for the big games. I worked well with him I think. With some guys it just clicks."

"For Ray, it's all about consistency," says linesman Brad Kovachik, "in approach, in performance, and in love of the game. Every game was big, and every game was fun, because he was a pro. I always go back to what Ray said to me eight or nine years ago. We were doing a game in Toronto at the Gardens, *Hockey Night in Canada*, Maple Leafs versus Canadiens. During the national anthem, he was standing next to me and he said, "Saturday night in Maple Leaf Gardens. Where else would you rather be?"

Fighters and Brawlers

*It's easy to be an official when you don't have a whistle
and a striped shirt on.*
—Harry Neale, TV commentator, NHL coach 1978–1985

A few years ago, while working a game in New Jersey, Scampy
was escorting Maple Leaf Tie Domi to the penalty box after
a fight when he noticed Domi's jersey was torn.

"Tie, your jersey is all ripped up there," Scampy ob-
served.

Domi started to take it off as he sat down. "You want it?"
he asked Ray.

"Jeez, yeah!" Scampy was never one to turn down an
addition to his memorabilia collection, so Scampy took the
jersey, skated over, and gave it to the Toronto equipment guy.
A few moments later, the same guy came back with a new
jersey for Domi, and Ray skated it back over to the box.

"You think you'd want to autograph that jersey for me?"
Scampy asked.

"Absolutely. I'll see you after the game," Domi replied.

The Leafs ended up getting waxed, but the outcome
didn't make a difference to Domi. A promise is a promise.

There are usually one or two guards outside the officials'
room, just in case a crazy fan, or an angry player, coach, or
GM decides to make a visit. Obviously on this occasion,

Domi's body language was non-threatening when he came to see Scampy.

"After the game, we're sitting in our dressing room, with guards outside the door, and Domi just walks in," Scampy says, "and Andy Van Hellemond, our boss at the time, was in the room for a visit."

"Hey Scamp, here's your jersey," Domi announced. He flipped it to Scampy, who looked out of the corner of his eye over at Van Hellemond.

"Thanks, Tie," said Scampy.

"Big night," Domi continued. "Check out the signature." The sweater was autographed and underneath Domi's name it read: "March 1, 2002. 3,000 penalty minutes."

"Wow. Thank you, Tie...congratulations on the monumental achievement," Scampy said with a laugh. Scampy's a big fan of the fights, and he loves the heavyweights.

"They go, they break it up, they say something, and they're on their way," Scampy explains.

It's the only time on the ice when an official can kind of be a fan. Of course, the refs and linesmen still have to keep an eye on the other players, and on the cleanliness of the bout, but it's really the only chance they get to focus in and enjoy the action.

"I never really took a poll or anything, but I think most of the officials enjoy the fights," Scampy says. "Especially the older guys. It's part of the game; it was part of hockey growing up."

It's amazing that in a society inundated with knives and guns, stabbings and shootings, hockey gets criticized for good, old-fashioned, mano-a-mano bouts: Men sorting out their anger the traditional way, without weapons, but with fists. Nevertheless, beyond that hypocrisy, there is a relatively strong effort to eliminate pugilism from puck. Among officials, former linesman Kevin Collins had a reputation for discouraging the fights. He'd often jump in early to break up a bout, much to the dismay of the crowd. Collins is now an NHL officiating manager.

Under normal circumstances there are three criteria for stopping a fight: if it's a mismatch right from the start, if one guy gets a clear advantage, or if either one falls to the ice. In three-plus decades, Scampy has seen, and broken up, his fair share of donnybrooks.

It's tough to pick out one "toughest guy," but according to Scampy, pound for pound, Domi is right up there. He also ranks Bob Probert high on the list.

"Probert's a big man, with a big reach," Scampy recalls. "He'd pull you in, drill you a few times, push you outside his range, get his wind, then pull you back in and drill you a few more times."

"Probert would rag doll guys," linesman Mark Pare adds, "because he had such good leverage. He'd push 'em and pull 'em. McSorley would do that, too. Probert's teammate Joey Kocur … I was on the ice, Detroit against Boston, when he punched Jay Miller's helmet and cracked it. What a puncher. I mean, at those moments, you're an official and a fan."

"Even though he had some chemical problems, Probert's a great guy off the ice," Scampy adds. "Probert and Kocur together in Detroit were scary. You should see Kocur's knuckles. Man, he's gonna have some serious arthritis some day. Big meat hooks, and a tough, tough, tough, guy."

Referee Bill McCreary officiated the famous Domi/Probert II fight. Domi, then of the Rangers, had pulled off a surprise win against Probert late in the 1991–92 season. The brash "Albanian Assassin," who skated away from the fight pretending to put on a championship boxing belt, had less than seventy-five NHL games on his résumé.

The heavily publicized rematch came on December 2, 1992, at Madison Square Garden. The NHL wasn't overly thrilled with the ink leading up to it. The New York and Detroit newspapers had the "tale of the tape" the morning of the game, featuring profiles of the combatants. The two fighters didn't disappoint. About a dozen seconds into the game, their gloves hit the ice just off the center ice face-off circle.

"Get back boys, we're going to enjoy this ourselves," McCreary remembers saying to bystanders. Domi landed the single biggest punch, but Probert dominated the rest of the fight. On the Detroit bench, as the two skated off, the usually reserved Steve Yzerman mocked Domi, mimicking his championship belt maneuver. Despite a one-sided outcome, the New York fans gave both men a standing ovation for a lengthy battle.

"There's some great personalities in the fight part of the game," Scampy declares. "You'll often hear people say that the biggest tough guys are often the nicest guys off the ice. It's true a lot of times. They're sweethearts off the ice, like Domi, always making an effort with charities and such. There's a bunch of guys like that. These guys can be pretty funny, too. Serious business. Funny guys."

Referee turned League executive Stephen Walkom was working in New York one night in 2003 when Darren Langdon of the Canadiens was anxious to jump into a fight already underway.

"Hey, take it easy," Walkom warned Langdon as he jockeyed in the corner. "Don't worry about it. Your team's already on the power play."

Without blinking, Langdon answered, "I don't give a shit, *I'm* not on the power play!" Walkom actually laughed out loud, and Langdon remained out of the skirmish.

Speaking of New York, Garry Howatt, back with the Islanders, was another talented scrapper, and he wasn't much taller than Scampy. Howatt played in the NHL from 1972 to 1984.

"This was when hair pulling was within reason," Scampy remembers, "and Howatt used to go for the hair a lot. Pull a guy down and just drill him. That part wasn't so funny, especially for the guy getting hit."

When most long-time officials talk about no-nonsense toughness, a different Islander name comes to mind.

"The best fighter, I think, was Clark Gillies, although I only got to see him up close once," remembers Wayne Bonney.

"I'd agree with that," says Leon Stickle. "Garry Howatt and Tiger Williams, those two would take on anyone, but the toughest guy overall was Gillies."

"One of the strongest people I ever saw was Clark Gillies," adds former referee Terry Gregson, "the guy I'd most want to avoid. It was best to leave him alone. I saw him wake up once or twice, and he sure could handle himself. Aside from that, he was a class guy and a solid hockey player."

"He was a massive man in his heyday," adds McCreary. "Gentle giant? Forget that … maybe if you left him alone."

By the time linesman Mark Pare joined the NHL, Clark Gillies didn't have to fight much.

"He was left alone by the time I got to the league," Pare says, "but he was tough. The most amazing fight I saw early on was his teammate Bob Nystrom and Scott Stevens when he first came up with Washington. It was like watching two cartoon characters; they just whaled away. Both of their heads would snap back from a punch and then come forward and they'd just keep whaling. They traded punches for forty-five seconds continuously. I was standing there with Ron Foyt and I just couldn't believe it … you're smiling to yourself thinking, 'this is unreal.'

"Eventually, the two of them were leaning forehead to forehead out of exhaustion, and when Foyt asked, 'Are you two done?', they started laughing. They were so whipped they couldn't move, and they were holding each other up. After we peeled them apart, I took Nystrom and started toward the box and he said, 'I'm not going there, forget that.' We skated to the gate for the dressing room." Nystrom wanted a legitimate rest.

What most amazed Pare was the condition the two players were in, to be able to fight like that and then be able to stand up, let alone skate off.

"Now, that was a good fight," Pare re-emphasizes.

Stickle remembers a Nystrom classic as well.

"Eddie Kea, who played in Atlanta, fought Bob Nystrom," Stickle reminisces. "The Islanders were coming into their own, and so was Nystrom, apparently. It was the longest, toughest, up-and-down fight that I saw in my whole career."

"Probert was tough," Stickle adds. "I had the Craig Cox/Probert rematch in Detroit; they had fought in Vancouver. The second one started down in the corner, went for awhile, and they broke themselves up. They were swung out."

~

Scampy remembers fights, fighters, and reputations.

During a thirteen-year career, Orland Kurtenbach played for the Rangers, Bruins, Leafs, and eventually Vancouver, and although he racked up fewer penalty minutes than games played, he had the distinction of being an extremely good fighter.

"That's what they say," Scampy points out, without identifying the omnipotent "they." "They say he was the best fighter ever, and I never had the chance to jump into one of his." Scampy's career began only three years before Kurtenbach's ended.

"This day and age, many believe Georges Laraque is the heavyweight champ. Tony Twist was [also] an exceptionally strong man," Scampy mentions. "Rob Ray was a big jersey puller, obviously—they call it the Rob Ray rule. He'd lose his own jersey. He never wore an undershirt, so the opponent never had anything to grab. The fight strap came about because of Rob Ray."

The Rob Ray rule penalizes a player for not having his "tie down" fastened. This fight strap is inside the jersey dangling along the small of the back and is supposed to be clipped to a player's pants. If it comes loose, accidentally or intentionally, the player with the undone strap gets a game misconduct. Rob Ray used to immediately take off his jersey during a fight so his opponent would have nothing to grab on to. It was considered unfair, dangerous because of the advantage, and for some, a bit too much bravado. The rule was put in place to keep jerseys on.

"You let the heavyweights go about their business," Scampy explains spontaneously. "If you jump in before a fight starts, they're just going to get after it a few moments later. The pro fighters rarely, if ever, break the fight rules—gouge, pull hair, or head butt. They engage, fight, and break, and more often than not, they're exhausted."

$\sim$

The term "old-time hockey" for the most part means tough, no-holds-barred hockey. And tough, no-holds-barred hockey is what Scampy saw in the seventies. Current and future officials, barring a jarring reversal of trends down the road, will never have to deal with the old-time, bench-clearing brawls that defined the NHL thirty years ago. Until the league started handing out ejections, suspensions, and fines for leaving the bench in the early eighties, episodes of on-ice anarchy were common.

Probably the most publicized affair occurred in New York between the Rangers and Bruins on December 23, 1979. Scampy was one of the linesmen. The fight broke out after the game, once the Bruins had secured a 4–3 win.

"I went to the initial fight," Scampy says. "I was working on a scrap when a fan reached over and drilled Stan Jonathan. Uh-oh. All hell broke loose, I remember going to the players' bench and trying to pull players back."

"Jesus Christ guys, this is going to cost us a fortune," Scampy said at the time, referring to the potential heavy fines from the League office.

The brawl lasted fifteen minutes. The most memorable scene was one of Bruin Mike Milbury hitting a fan over the head with said fan's shoe.

"I was at that game," declares Scampy's long-time friend and Rangers fan Phil Shulman. "It was unbelievable."

Shulman saw a lot of Scampy's memorable moments at the Garden. He saw Scampy trip James Patrick, he watched the Rangers win the 1994 Stanley Cup, and he saw Scampy work the one game in which he actually got tired … really tired.

"Oh jeez," Scampy groans, "1992. Adam Graves slashed Mario Lemieux, Lemieux had a broken wrist, or at least pretended to have one, and the Penguins went crazy. We were out there forever. It was me, Ron Finn, and

Andy Van Hellemond was the ref. Fight after fight after fight. Graves was suspended, even though I think he hit Lemieux by accident, and the thing went on forever."

"It was the only time Scampy ever looked really tired after a game," Shulman reinforces. "We went out for pizza and he was fried. I remember looking at the box score. It was about a foot long."

The mid-seventies Philadelphia Flyers, the "Broad Street Bullies," were no strangers to long box scores. They made brawls a serious part of their act.

"Matt Pavelich likes to say he saved a guy's life," Scampy points out. "Some guy hacked Bobby Clarke and got a penalty, and all the Flyers went after this guy. In fact, two or three Flyers went over the boards, into the penalty box, and started pummeling this guy. Somehow, Pavelich got over top of him and Matt was taking the brunt of the punches. They weren't trying to deliberately hurt Matt, but he took several punches while he was trying to save this guy. They went a thousand miles an hour, Don Saleski, Ed Van Imp, Dave Schultz, and Bob Kelly."

Their ultimate bash came on October 25, 1974, in Oakland California against the Seals, with linesmen Leon Stickle and Ryan Bozak and referee Bryan Lewis.

"The shit hit the fan and it was unbelievable," Stickle remembers. "I think Mike Christie hit Bobby Clarke in the head with his stick, and cut him. The Flyers lost it. It went on forever and ever and ever. Both benches were completely unloaded, and we ended up in the stands. They weren't drawing very well in Oakland, but they loved the

Flyers, and they loved the brawls. Philly was the big draw everywhere because they were a good hockey club, the champs at the time, and were well noted for the bruising style. I think it was also during a fairly extensive road trip so they probably weren't in a great mood."

Seals defenseman Ted McAneeley remembers being held in a headlock by Ed Van Imp at one end of the ice, away from the melee.

"He was trying to gouge my eyes out," McAneeley recalls.

"You go to the place where the fire ignited and try to get that sorted out, but on a night like that, you're just at their mercy," explains Stickle. "You try to go where the worst part of it is, but when you get fans involved, players are coming through the penalty box trying to get up into the stands. You actually pray a lot. I remember it like it was yesterday. You don't really have a clue what's going on around you because there's so much going on. In this particular case, when you break up two guys, and move on, those two guys will just go back at it, because there was no penalty box to put them in—there were already fights in the penalty box. It was like the Wild West: ten gunfights going on at one time, and eventually you just try to duck the bullets yourself."

In general, Stickle, Scampy, and the other linesmen of the era attempted to take a pragmatic approach to brawl break-ups. Scampy's stature wasn't a problem. With his low center of gravity, he could get up between the guys, grab one player's arms, and move him away. He had leverage, plus, a lot of times, any last-second punches would be over his head.

"Back during the brawls, as a linesman you'd take the worst-case scenario, either the first fight, or the one that developed as the wildest. You'd grab two guys, deal with them, get them to the box, and then come back and pick two more. You'd always go back to the worst-cast scenario. It wasn't like every time you had five choices; you'd usually have at least one sensible guy or pair that was just waltzing around the ice to stay out of the fray. Then again, you'd get the occasional deal where a guy standing around gets sucker punched. We never tried to go in alone. You'd both go in and break the one up, then both come back for the next. If you go alone and grab one guy, the other guy can still punch.

"Refs would very rarely reach in; they had to keep an eye out for other infractions. By the time you'd get done with two fights, the rest of them would usually be exhausted. The boring part was standing around waiting for them to figure out the penalties, although it was a real nice time to rest."

Like Stickle, Bryan Lewis remembers the Oakland brawl like it was yesterday.

"Someone sent me a picture from that night," Lewis says. "I'm sitting on top of the boards, pen and paper in hand, writing down numbers. I'll never forget Jimmy "the Chief" Neilson coming to the aide of Christie, who was absolutely pummeled. I don't think Christie was ever the same after that, poor kid. When he went to blow his nose the next day, he must have had to reach around the back of his head. Actually, it was Bobby Clarke who finally put an end to that brawl. He yelled, 'That's enough, boys,' and it was like the Red Sea parted. It was over."

"We were doing reports after that game until 2:30 in the morning," Stickle remembers. "Everything was hand-written. Then we had to fly and meet with [NHL President Clarence] Campbell." There was no VP of Hockey Operations in those days. Campbell was the judge and jury for fines and suspensions.

The teams set an NHL record with 232 penalty minutes, with 144 of them belonging to the Flyers. (The Seals won the game, 4–1, then went winless in their next seven.)

The next day, referee Lewis was in Vancouver, with the Canucks hosting Philadelphia.

"Flyers goalie Bobby Taylor stopped me in the hall before the game," Lewis recalls. "He said to me, 'You don't have to worry about 'em emptying tonight. They've got seatbelts on the benches.'"

Campbell, who preferred holding hearings and doling out punishment in person, called the catalysts of the brawl to the League offices for face-to-face meetings. It wasn't the first time for a number of Flyers. Three of them were suspended.

"They worked like a pack of hyenas," Scampy marvels. "They'd pick a guy, and they'd just mug him. They were fearless. Plus, they'd take their penalties, and just kill them off. It would be one thing if they gave up a ton of goals shorthanded, but they didn't. They could get away with smashing guys and not give up goals. I'm sure [coach

Fred] Shero would have changed tactics if the crazy stuff cost them games, but why change?" Over four seasons, from 1973 to 1977, Bobby Clarke scored eighteen short-handed goals, while Rick MacLeish tallied nine.

"We used to hear about the Philadelphia flu," Scampy continues. "I'm not sure if anyone ever claimed injury or illness so they didn't have to play Philly, particularly in Philly, but I'm sure they thought about it. It was said the visiting dressing room at the Spectrum was the quietest dressing room in sports—a lot of nerves."

The Flyers' fearless attitude extended to the officials, with whom they showed little respect.

"I threw Bob Clarke out of a face-off one night," Scampy recalls, "and he said, 'Just drop the puck. Nobody f——king came here to watch you tonight.' Some guys you can talk to, mention something to, albeit very briefly, but not Clarke. He was all business and super competitive: 'You do your job and I'll do mine.' I don't have a problem with that." Scampy adds, "He's a great story. He wasn't drafted, fought with diabetes, and he was captain of an NHL champion."

Long-time referee Wally Harris loved to let things go, which was a perfect fit for games involving the Flyers.

"I had them twenty-three times one year," Harris recalls with amazement. "I was thinking, holy moly, did everyone else retire? But I enjoyed those types of games. I liked the hard games. Once things got a little crazy, I was glad to have Scampy and [John] D'Amico as linesmen. They learned how to cool things down. It's amazing the benefit of two good linesmen; they save you a lot of trouble."

Eventually, the officials' association came up with the idea of heavy fines for bench-clearing brawls. The League adopted it, and for the most part, the outrageous donny-brooks went the way of the dodo.

"One guy I really admire is Jack McIlhargey," Scampy adds as a Flyers postscript. "He was with the Flyers around their heyday, he mugged people, beat up people when he was in Philly, and then he got traded to the Canucks."

Scampy lined McIlhargey's first game against his old team, played in Vancouver.

"Now we'll see how tough this guy is. He's got nobody to back him up," Scampy said that day in the officials' room.

"He ran Bob Clarke all night long, and nobody came near him. From that day on, I had a lot respect for Jack. He was on his own out there, and he was fearless. They either had a lot of respect for him or they were paranoid of him."

Paranoid would be a good description of players and officials around Steve Durbano, who skated with four different NHL clubs between 1972 and 1979.

"He was something," Scampy declares. "I remember him with Pittsburgh. You never knew what he was going to do. I remember him getting thrown out of a game. He left the ice [and] there were still fights going on, so he climbed back up over the boards and glass and got back on the ice and started fighting again, still in his gear."

The late Durbano also played forty-five games for Birmingham in the World Hockey Association in 1977–78, and racked up a league-leading 284 penalty minutes.

The WHA was no stranger to brawl-fests. There was less talent across the board than in the NHL, and the emphasis of the upstart league was to entertain the fans and bring them back by any means necessary. The league lasted from 1972 to 1979.

"My first game after spending time in the minors was a WHA game, Hartford Whalers hosting the Minnesota Fighting Saints," linesman Wayne Bonney remembers. "I was with Pierre Belanger, and the ref was Alan Glaspel, out of Oshawa. Our boss at the time was former NHL referee Vern Buffy.

"It was an all-out brawl. One of the Carlson boys, Jack, the brother of the guys who played the Hansen Brothers, is runnin' around like a maniac. We're chasing him all over. Jack goes into the benches. I go into the benches. I had forty minutes chasing Jack. Pierre's running everywhere else. I think we had three hundred minutes in the first and part of the second; then it quieted down in the third. There were only two fights late in the game. So Buffy comes into the officials' room after the game."

"Great game, boys! Alan, you did such a good job, I'll write the report," Buffy said, according to Bonney. The officials looked puzzled.

"Buffy hadn't shown up for the first and second period," Bonney remembers. "He only wrote up the two fights that he saw in the third period. The next day he was fired. There were only two fights?! Try about a *hundred* and two."

Although NHL referees are responsible for handing out punishment for infractions and fights, it doesn't mean they're not fond of the fisticuffs.

"I've had the privilege of seeing a lot of great fights," declares former referee and now NHL Director of Officiating Steve Walkom. "I think spontaneous fighting is a great part of our game. I think staged fights should evolve their way out of the game, and I think that's happening. You have to be able to play."

Walkom's most memorable recent fight involved Ryan VandenBussche of Chicago against another middleweight in Tampa Bay.

"It lasted like two minutes," Walkom remembers. "They really got into it and blood was flying everywhere. VandenBussche puts a lot into his fights."

Walkom used to work in the Ontario Hockey League, where young scrappers work hard to leave a mark.

"When I was there, Derian Hatcher and Eric Lindros were in the League, and they were great fighters in juniors. They used to have some epic fisticuffs."

NHL referee Rob Shick worked his way up through the American League, and remembers the ultimate in bad public relations.

"I remember it was boy scouts day in Springfield," Shick recalls. "They had 5,000 boy scouts in the building for Springfield against Fredericton. Freddie Lane was coaching Springfield, and he ended up going over and punching the other coach. It was unbelievable. Must have been traumatic for some, but it actually turned out to be kind of funny."

Speaking of coaches who join the fray, Harry Neale, Scampy's good friend and now a respected and entertaining TV commentator, couldn't help himself once while coaching the Vancouver Canucks in the early eighties.

"I got tossed in Quebec City," Neale says. "Wilf Paiement of the Nordiques had Tiger Williams pinned to the boards, just down from the bench. In that rink, you could walk off the bench into the seats. So, while Williams is pinned, a fan comes down the aisle and takes a swing at him. I left the bench to try to get the fan. I was thrown out and suspended for six games.

"Roger Neilson was my assistant," Neale continues. "He filled in for me and won all six games. At that point I said, 'Just take over for me now.' I was going to be the GM anyway. We went all the way to the finals before losing in four straight to the Islanders."

One never knows what one's misbehavior might sprout.

Neale expresses strong opinions about the officials, and he should be allowed to, not necessarily because he's a national broadcaster, but because he used to be an official.

"I like them to take charge," Neale points out. "If I was yapping, and the ref said, 'One more and you're gone,' I'd shut up. Frankly, I wouldn't take the shit they take. I think they put up with way too much. In some cases, their best solution is to say, 'I screwed up.' That shuts up a player or coach faster than anything. As a coach, I'd try to make them laugh early in the game; go easy with some, and tough with others. If we got to know each other, we'd be more tolerant. Some coaches treat the officials like the enemy."

CHAPTER 3

Hall of Fame referee Andy Van Hellemond knew how to handle coaches possibly better than any referee in history.

"He didn't take any guff from them," Scampy declares, "and he was fair, and he was certainly good. He'd make sure they were informed on one hand, and on the other hand, he simply couldn't be intimidated. It didn't matter who the coach was, or their style; he could address them. He wouldn't hesitate to give out a bench minor."

Van Hellemond also had creative ways of dealing with players and fights.

"Once, in Detroit, it was Andy, Jerry Pateman, and me," remembers linesman Mark Pare. "The puck is inside the Detroit blue line, and everyone's running around trying to crush each other, slamming, banging."

"We're not going to have this all night," Van Hellemond told Pare.

"So, Andy orders us to take Lee Norwood of Detroit and Perry Turnball of St. Louis out to center ice," Pare says.

"You wanna fight, you wanna screw around," Van Hellemond said. The two linesmen looked at each other. "Get them out there!" Van Hellemond ordered.

The linesmen shoved the players out to center ice and the two went at it hard.

"The other players are looking around thinking, 'Holy cow, am I next?" Pare remembers. "There wasn't so much as a high stick the rest of the night; the whistle blew, and everyone disappeared like smoke."

"You wanna fight in Joe Louis's backyard, then let's go," Pare remembers Van Hellemond saying.

"Andy had a lot of tricks up his sleeve."

~

As for calling penalties related to fights, the rules have changed countless times, especially in the area of how much help the linesmen can offer. Since the institution of the two-referee system in 2000, the linesman's ability to help out with certain calls has been limited; the idea being that just as the refs do their jobs, the linesmen should focus on theirs.

The intent is to make for more ice coverage, to cover obstruction more closely while having an extra set of eyes for the gnarly stuff behind the play. It has also meant giving young referees a chance to partner up and learn from veteran officials.

"Now, linesmen can only call major penalties and bench minors," Scampy says. "They used to be able to assist on minor calls, or if blood was drawn."

Now, hypothetically, if a linesman sees someone spear a guy in the back of the leg, and the ref misses it, the linesman can't call it. Even if the guy who gets speared turns around, drops the gloves, and beats up the spearing perpetrator, the linesman still can't mention the spear.

"If the guy who did the spearing turtles," Scampy points out, "his team might end up with a five-minute power play. A coach might say, 'Scampy, you saw that—you saw the spear.' Yeah, I did, and there's not a damn thing I can do about it."

(Note: If a linesman deems the infraction to be serious enough to warrant a "match" penalty, he can report it

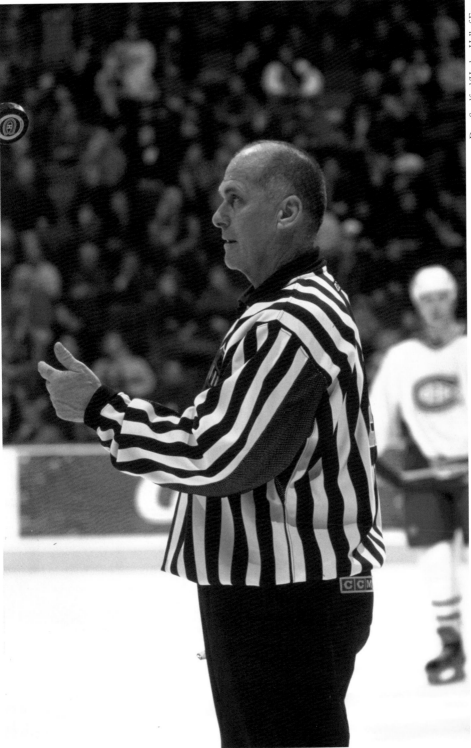

Scampy, #53.

A young Ray Scapinello (age 11), when he was still known as "Gus" rather than "Scampy."

Scapinello training to be a linesman at the Bruce Hood School of Officiating (1968).

NHL officials' training camp, late '70's. Ray is first on the left in the front row. Also included in this group of cohorts are three men who went on to head up the officials for the NHL. Bryan Lewis is in the back row, third from the left; in the same row, Andy Van Hellemond is sixth from the left; John McCauley is in the front, sixth from the left; and Ray's early mentor and legendary linesman, the late John D'Amico, is second from the right in the front.

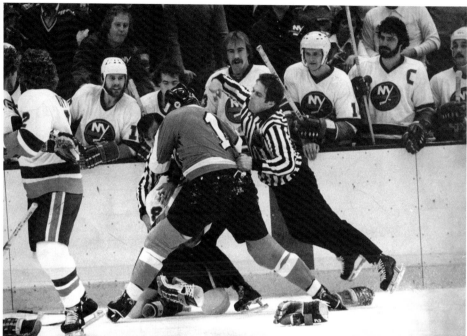

In a career that spanned four decades in the NHL, Scampy broke up his share of fights, from bench brawls, to the Broad Street Bullies, to the more run-of-the-mill melees. Here, he throws himself into the action.

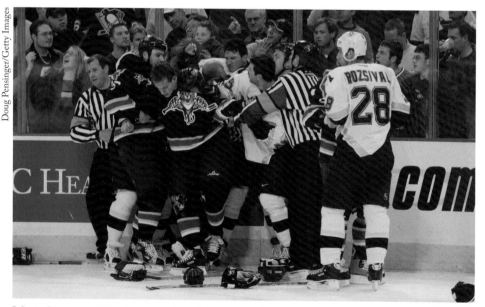

Mario Lemieux #66 of the Pittsburgh Penguins, back center, is restrained by linesman Ray Scapinello (the bald head in the middle of the action) after a fight with Brad Ference #45 of the Florida Panthers at the Mellon Arena on February 6, 2003, in Pittsburgh.

Ready for the face-off, early in his career.

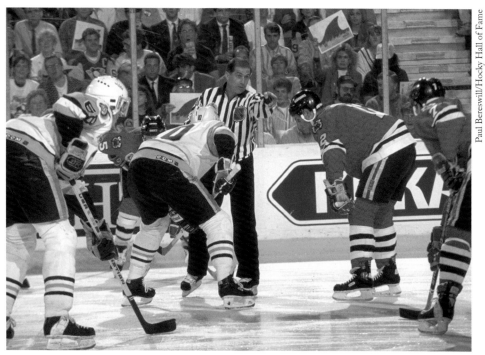

Taking control of the face-off circle.

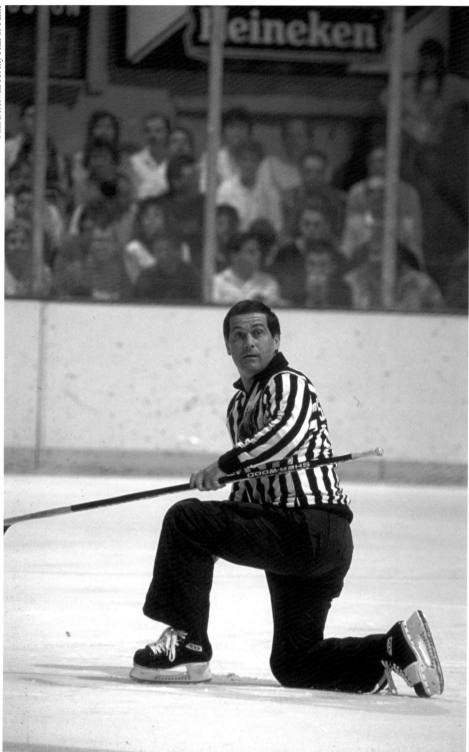

Is that another stick for your collection, Scampy?

At 5-foot-7, Scapinello was always on the ice, and in the middle of brawls, with players much bigger than him. Here he escorts Mario Lemieux, captain of the Pittsburgh Penguins, to the penalty box.

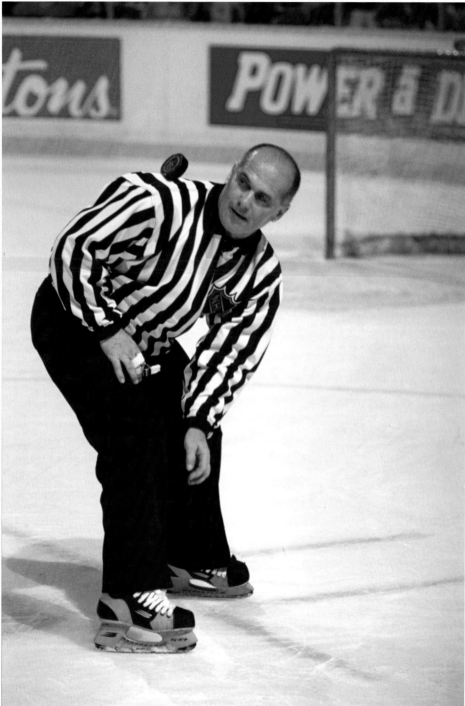

Incoming! Despite all the spills, punches, pucks and knocks he took over his long career, Scampy never missed a single game due to injury, illness, or anything else.

to a referee. A match penalty means the guilty party gets tossed out of the game, usually for intent to injure.)

The League put the onus on the two referees to see everything.

"I prefer being able to help out," Scampy adds. "I've been in a game when a guy gets high sticked and he's bleeding ..."

"Pat Quinn says, 'You were looking right at that, you saw that!' And I'll answer, 'Yeah, I saw that; he high-sticked him right in the face. Number 14, he clipped Darcy Tucker."

"'Well, tell the ref,' Quinn will demand. I'll tell him all night, and there's nothing he can do about it, I'll answer. 'Jesus Christ, what kind of call is that?'"

Ironically, if a supervisor is at the game and a player picks up nine stitches on something that wasn't called, the referees are going to hear about it.

"If two linesmen can do it, why can't two refs?" asks Stephen Walkom, a supporter of the two-ref system. "Over time, you'd think two sets of eyes were better than one: Enforce obstruction and have the right angles. Under the three-man (one ref, two linesmen), we gave too many re-sponsibilities to linesmen. The game is so fast now. I think this put the focus back on the linesmen to do what they're really supposed to do, and improves the flow of the game. Linesmen had become mini-refs."

Prior to the two-ref system, referees were *supposed* to listen to their linesmen, and learn. It was a fight situation in 1997 that allowed referee Paul Devorski to learn a hard lesson about being young and headstrong, and Scampy was one of his teachers.

"Back when Detroit and Colorado used to kick the shit out of each other," Devo remembers, "[Claude] Lemieux had laid waste to [Kris] Draper along the boards during the '96 playoffs in Colorado."

It was Game Six of the Western Conference Finals when Lemieux hit Draper from behind. Draper fractured his jaw, suffered a broken nose, and had severe facial lacerations. Lemieux was fined a thousand bucks and suspended for the first two games of the Cup Finals against Florida.

"The following year," Devorski continues, "I had the first game back in Detroit, against Colorado, the first game back there since the Draper thing. The first period was going along great, but with about five minutes left in it, Larionov and Forsberg get into it. They get tied up and start to fight, and we knew then we were in for some trouble, because when did you see Larionov ever fight?

"So everyone's watching that, and then McCarty circles the wagons. He knew Lemieux was out there. I was watching the other altercation. I guess McCarty just skated around all of the players to Lemieux, who sees him coming, and Lemieux turtles, and McCarty just lays a beating on him. He was pounding him, and there was a pool of blood under Lemieux. Now, Shanahan and Foote go at it at center ice, and then Roy and Vernon skate out to center ice and go toe-to-toe."

It was a good, old-fashioned line brawl, goalies included.

"I have the tape," Devo continues, "and my boy will say, 'Hey Dad, let's watch the fight tape.' Well, this gives me the chance to actually see what happened and what I was looking at."

Devorski's problem didn't really stem from the mayhem itself. It stemmed from his stubbornness in handling it.

"I didn't want to throw the goalies out; they were the secondary fight. Had it been now, they would have been tossed for sure (for starting a secondary fight and for crossing center ice). So, they're cut up, and their equipment is all over. I give the goalies ten minutes each—misconducts, no fights. They thought they were done, they were on the bench going to the room, and I said, 'No, no, get back in the net.'"

Meanwhile, Scampy had skated over to grab McCarty, and started to pull him aside, assuming he'd get thrown out.

"I hadn't seen anything there, 'til the final end of it, and I see him standing over Lemieux, so I say, 'Get him in the box.' Scampy's pretty urgent. He's in my face saying, 'Devo, you gotta get rid of this guy, you gotta get rid of this guy,' and I'm thinking to myself, I didn't see it all … nah … put him in the box."

Devorski gave McCarty a double minor for roughing and a ten-minute misconduct. Colorado had a four-minute power play, when, as Devo admits later, they should have had a five-minute power play and McCarty should have received a game misconduct.

"I keep McCarty in the game, and [Colorado coach Marc] Crawford's going ape-shit on me," Devo remembers.

In the officials' room, Scampy and fellow linesman Dan Schachte expressed their concerns.

"Devo, this guy kicked the shit out of him," Scampy said. "Jeez!"

"Well, too late now," Devorski responded. "Let's get this thing going again and wrap it up."

Devorski's decision came back to haunt him later in the evening.

"Wouldn't you know, the game goes into overtime, and who scores the winning goal … Darren McCarty. They must have loved me in Colorado. I had [Avalanche GM] Pierre Lacroix standing there in front of my door when I got off the ice giving me the business."

League Vice President Jim Gregory visited the room after the game. He asked the ref why McCarty hadn't been tossed and was clearly upset with the decision, although he did commend Devo for keeping the goalies in the game.

"I'll never forget that night. I should have listened. I've got two senior linesmen. From that day on, it was 'Scampy, whatever you tell me.' I was young, cocky, thought I knew it all."

Devo points out that had the brawl happened today, with the rule changes made over time, the two goalies would have been tossed, Shanny and Foote would have been tossed, as would McCarty. Goalies are not allowed to cross the center ice red line for any reason, unless for an equipment problem or to get a drink during a TV time-out. A minor penalty results if they do. Shanahan and

Foote would have been tossed because secondary altercations are not allowed in the NHL. Once one fight starts, the rest of the gents better cool their jets.

"Today, we just couldn't do it," Devo says. "You mean to tell me those two goalies didn't fight? I tell you what, though, it's a fun fight tape to watch."

~

Missed or screwed up calls are one thing. Dangerous fight moments are harder to forget.

"I was on the ice when [Nick] Kypreos got knocked out," Scampy recalls. "That was scary. And I saw another guy get knocked out, and punched again while he was falling unconscious—that was maybe the scariest moment ever. They were both legitimate square-offs, nothing dirty or cheap. Very rare to see something like that out of a regular fight."

Usually, the nasty stuff comes out of fights between guys who aren't used to fighting—players who don't usually drop the gloves are the ones most likely to do something dirty or unexpected.

Nasty language is another byproduct of conflict. Most of the foul atrocities that come out of fighters' mouths are not suitable for these pages. Scampy recalls something typical that doesn't involve someone's wife or mother: "I'll rip your arm off and beat you over the head with it."

"Actually, a lot of the stuff is pretty funny," Scampy concludes. "One night in Chicago, I remember the Sutter brothers getting into it. Darryl [one of six Sutters from Viking, Alberta to play in the NHL] got into a scrap with one of the twins [Rich or Ron]. The shit hit the fan in the corner, there's pushing and some milling, and Darryl says to his brother, 'Get the hell out of here right now, or I'll kick the shit out of you like I do when we're at home.'"

Fight humor comes in many forms. Wayne Bonney's wife worked for Fletcher Leisure Group in Montreal when they were still in business distributing Leaf underwear. This was originally the stuff that was supposed to pull sweat away from a person's body, keeping them warm and insulated. Many of the officials wore it.

"Ron Asselstine was a pretty big guy," Bonney smiles, "and all my wife had for him that fit was one set of bright red underwear. So as Asselstine is breaking up a fight, he falls, and a guy's skate comes down and cuts right through his pants and the protective padding underneath ... just enough to split the pants and pad and expose the underwear. Ron falls back, collects himself, and looks at his leg. Then he starts screaming, 'Aaahhhhhh, shit, I'm bleeeeeding ... ahhh, I'm gonna bleed to death!' The trainer came out, took a look, and said, 'That's your underwear.'"

"Asselstine is one of a number of characters involved in the sport," Scampy says. "The personalities are one of the great constants that go with hockey. Fighting itself brings a personality to the game. Even though now it's pretty miniscule, it's part of the game and it always has been. It's part of the sport's history and I hope it never goes away."

Young "Gus" Grows

Scotty, there's something else. I've seen some of these new officials.
When are you going to hire men, and stop hiring midgets?
—NHL President Clarence Campbell to Referee-in-Chief
Scotty Morrison, autumn 1971

Back in the forties and fifties, between Guelph and Hespeler in Ontario, there was a quarry community called Glen Christie, population eighty. Domtar Corporation dynamited stone and made lime at the site. Ray's dad, George, or "Sonny," drove a front-loader. The Scapinello family, which included mom Dorothy, older sister Dianne, Ray, and younger brother Dougie, lived in a company home.

"There were about twenty simple houses and all of the residents were employees of Domtar," Scampy explains.

Shopping meant going to Guelph or Hespeler about fifteen minutes in either direction, because Glen Christie wasn't a real town. It was born and it died with the quarry.

Ray attended classes at a one-room schoolhouse. The school handled grades one through eight, all in one class with one teacher, and little Ray Scapinello wasn't much of a student.

"I'd run out and shoot pool every day after school. Wasn't much for reading or homework. I'm not sure, but I think I may have repeated a couple of grades," Scampy laughs.

Although Ray didn't hit the books very hard as a youngster, he was absolutely no slouch when it came to doing actual labor. As a twelve-year-old, Ray spent his summer working at a tobacco farm in Drumbo with two friends, Doug and Don Gee. They suckered tobacco, which meant they separated the sucker between the stalk and the actual tobacco leaf.

"We'd do two rows at a time, and get paid a certain amount by the acre. We were demons. We became really good at it," Scampy says. They eventually put together some decent money, and Scampy gave all of his earnings to his mother.

"It was all cash and she'd put it in the bank for me," Scampy explains. Or so he thought.

Scampy's sister, Dianne, worked at Royal Bank in Guelph. Mrs. Scapinello was supposed to be putting Ray's money into an account there, but at the end of that summer, Ray found out the money was gone.

"I went to visit my sister and asked to see my passbook. I looked inside and there was nothing in there," Ray says, reliving the shock.

"Where did my money go? Where did *all* my money go?"

Ray's mom had spent the cash. She said the family needed it. Ray didn't see a dime, but he gradually realized that everyone had to work to help out the family.

CHAPTER 4

~

As the Glen Christie quarry expanded, the dynamiting shook and damaged the company houses and the families were forced to relocate. Scampy's family moved to Guelph when he was thirteen years old.

"All of my parents' friends were from Hespeler, but we decided to move the other direction to Guelph. I have no reason why." Glen Christie sat between the two towns, about 12 kilometers west to Hespeler and 20 kilometers east to Guelph.

The move created an inconvenience for Ray the hockey player, as he played most of his junior hockey in Hespeler.

"I started when I was five or six," Ray points out, "and I was a yapper, a real shift disturber."

He was also an outstanding skater, thus the logical nicknames Scamp, Scampy, and Scamper for the little guy named Scapinello who could skate.

Previous to this well-known moniker, Ray as a small child was called Gus for no particular reason, at least not one that made sense. He was named after the old fireman on the *Leave It to Beaver* television show from the fifties. Ray didn't look like Gus, or even sound like him, but someone decided to call him Gus all the same.

"I don't know what that was all about. Gus was, like, a thousand years old," Ray chuckles. "I know you go way back with me if I hear you calling me Gus."

As his youth hockey career burgeoned, so did the new name Scampy.

"I played peewee and bantam in Hespeler and then latched on to a travel team in Guelph for midget," Scampy remembers. "Back then they had a juvenile hockey setup that doesn't exist anymore. If you're of juvenile age now, which is seventeen, you'd be playing junior-A or junior-B if you're any good at all. Back then, midget hockey was good hockey, for fourteen- or fifteen-year-olds and up. There wasn't junior-B then."

As a cocky teenager who agitated opponents, and weighed 140 pounds soaking wet, Scampy needed protection on the ice.

"A couple guys on my hockey team were massive," Scampy says with amazement. "Bill Fox … he had to be six foot two when he was seventeen years old, but he was a real mild-mannered guy for the most part. He and a couple other guys looked after me. I could say what I wanted, when I wanted to, and these guys were well known to mop up if they were needed.

"Early in a playoff round, one guy cross-checked Fox and knocked out a few of his teeth," Scampy continues. "There was no way in a million years he could play in the next game, but our coach dressed him and put him on the end of the bench. Every time the guy who hit him would come onto the ice, Bill would stand up like he was going to come on, and the guy would go straight to his bench. I don't think either one of them played a shift."

Once, when Ray was going for a pre-practice twirl in Guelph, Philadelphia Flyers scout Marcel Pelletier saw him skate and briefly expressed interest.

CHAPTER 4

"Can you skate like that with a stick in your hand?" Pelletier asked.

"Absolutely," Scampy answered. "I just can't control the puck."

When Scampy was twenty years old, his career with the Guelph Platers wrapped up. Next, he joined a senior league team called the Guelph Regals. Despite being able to skate like the wind, Scampy spent most of the time on the end of the bench, since he was a twenty-one-year-old, and most of the players were more talented and experienced in their late twenties and early thirties. The next year the team folded, and the little right winger realized his hockey playing career had officially ended.

~

One oddity carried over from Scampy's youth hockey days all the way through his professional officiating career: his parents' lack of involvement in his passion.

"You know what seems a bit strange? My parents never once drove me to hockey. In fact, my parents never witnessed one of my NHL games. Not one. My dad didn't know a thing about hockey and didn't care," Ray explains. "He was working, and I was working. Simple as that.

"I had a beautiful collection of hockey sticks early in my NHL career. I came home one day and all of the sticks were cut in half, holding up the tomato plants."

These were vintage sticks from the early seventies—twigs autographed by Phil Esposito and Bobby Hull, cut in half with plants tied to them. They hadn't been displayed;

Ray had tucked them away in a crawl space. His father obviously found them.

"Do you realize what you've done?" Scampy thought at the time.

"Old school" is an oft-overused term these days. Ray's parents however, were indeed old school.

"My father was an old-fashioned Italian who worked his fanny off," Ray says. "My mother was a dutiful wife who took care of business at home. She raised the kids, cooked food for her husband when he came home midday, and later cooked the family dinner."

North America was a much different place back then. Ray's parents never took a vacation. For them, a vacation was driving to Hespeler to play cards with their friends on a Saturday afternoon. George was in bed at eight o'clock every night. He worked his butt off for twelve hours a day at the quarry, retired at sixty-one, and then worked another twenty-five years at a local golf club, the Cutten Club in Guelph.

"My dad, he's retired, he's driving my mom crazy, and he can't stand not working, so I helped him get a job at the golf club," Ray says. "I played at the Cutten Club and talked to the superintendent, Richard Creed. I asked him if he was looking for new employees."

"Who's looking?" Richard asked.

"My father," Ray said.

Ray's dad worked five days a week cutting the rough and the fairway and driving materials around.

George loved it. He thought he'd died and gone to heaven. The only big problem he had was his lack of golf etiquette.

"He didn't know squat about golf," Ray says. "He would be driving around while people were trying to hit. Someone would be hitting off the tee and he'd drive right past them. If he saw me, even while someone was teeing up, he'd yell, "Hey, Raymond!"

He was a tough guy in good health until the two-packs-a-day smoking habit finally caught up with him. When he was eighty-five, a year before his second retirement, George first heard the "C" word. When he was diagnosed with cancer, the doctor said, "We know you're mid-eighties, but you can still have an operation to try to stem it off."

George asked, "Can I go without the operation?"

The doctor said, "Yeah."

George responded, "See you later. I gotta go to work."

Ray's dad never did anything about the illness. A year later, in 2001, the cancer hit him hard and he was dead within two months. He had worked hard, raised a family, and left things better off for the next generation.

"To the day my dad died he kind of thought I was a bum because I was in hockey and I didn't work during the summer," Ray tells it.

When Scampy's father passed away, a few of the younger NHL officials showed up at the funeral home out of respect for Scampy. A group of family and friends were standing in the basement. Greg Kimmerly was there, along with Dean Warren and his wife, Diane. The group was having a nice chat when Maureen, Ray's wife, came down to get Scampy.

"Ray, the parish priest is here to say prayers. You gotta come up," Maureen said.

Ray's reaction was "Geez, I don't want to do that."

The group made its way upstairs and listened sullenly as the priest made his way through a version of preliminary funeral prayers. Some of the women wiped away tears. When the priest was finished, he offered anyone and everyone the opportunity to share their feelings.

"Does anyone want to share a story about Sonny?" the preacher asked. Everyone looked at Scampy. Scampy turned and looked at Greg Kimmerly.

"Greg, do you have a story for us?" Scampy inquired.

Kimmerly wouldn't know Scampy's dad if he tripped over him. The immediate look of shock and potential embarrassment that overcame Kimmerly's face subsided when Scampy flashed him a wry grin. Everyone had a good laugh and the room lightened up.

~

Dorothy Scapinello, Ray's mom, passed away in November of 2004 at age eighty-one, after living for a few years in a nursing home on a supportive care floor, suffering from dementia. She was safe and well taken care of, but the disease had robbed her of any clear thinking.

"A couple of years ago, my wife, Maureen, put a guest list in my mom's room," Ray says. "When a friend or family came for a visit, they would sign in and put down what time they were there."

Ray would pop in on a regular basis to visit and see who may have stopped by and signed the book.

"'Oh look, isn't that nice,' we'd say."

At one point, not so long before Mrs. Scapinello passed, Scampy's sister-in-law Marilyn, Doug's wife, came from Nova Scotia to Toronto to visit her own mother. During the trip, she made the extra effort to swing through Guelph to visit Dougie and Ray's mom.

"I didn't even know about it," Scampy says, "so on this particular day I go up a little after 2:00 to see Mom. I look at the book and it's signed Marilyn Scapinello, 11:00 a.m. to 2:00 p.m." Scampy had just missed her.

"Geez Mom, that was nice of Dougie's wife, Marilyn, to come visit you," Scampy said.

"Oh, too bad I missed her," his mom answered.

Scampy can hardly finish telling this story before he's laughing his fanny off.

"It's sad, but you have to laugh if not to cry," Scampy says, which reflects his outlook on everything: certain elements of life should be taken seriously, just not too seriously. The humor can be misleading. Although he didn't have what some might refer to as a "touchy-feely" relationship with his parents, Ray possesses an incredible amount of respect and love for both of them.

"Speaking of Mom," Scampy continues, "none of us look like her. I'm the spittin' image of my father, and the rest of us kind of look alike."

❦

Back when his professional hockey officiating career was just getting started, Ray's mother did him one big favor on a regular basis. Before making the NHL, Ray worked full-time at Canadian General Electric, and his mom helped him survive the job.

"I was working part-time officiating AHL games. My first season, I'd fly to Boston or wherever for the weekend, do a game Saturday and Sunday in Boston, Providence, or Springfield, and I wouldn't get back until Monday morning," Ray explains. "I could never get into work until after lunch on Mondays."

Ray's mom called in for him every Monday morning, saying he was sick. For five or six consecutive weeks she'd call in and tell them he was ill. Scampy's boss knew he officiated, and pulled him aside one day.

"Listen Ray, I understand you like officiating, but we pay you for a forty-hour week," the boss said. "We can't have you pulling in here every Monday afternoon. You're gonna have to make a decision."

"I understand. I respect that," Scampy answered. But he had one more weekend.

"This guy probably doesn't think I have the balls to pull this off one more time," Scampy thought.

So he pressed his luck.

"I flew and did the games, my mom called me in sick, I showed up in the afternoon, and that was it. The boss never said anything," Scampy says through a smile.

By the start of the following season Scampy was starting to work full-time in the NHL. This was good news for a lot of reasons, especially since the work at GE wasn't exactly up Ray's alley.

"I was working at General Electric minding my own business," Ray tells it, "working in the production control department. They made transformers, and to be honest, I don't know what I did." Scampy worked in the office, and it was his responsibility to order steel for the men who were building transformers. He was responsible for keeping up inventory records.

"Okay, so they're building transformer four, we need eighty yards of three-inch cold rolled steel," Scampy thinks back. "As the transformer is being built I'd say, 'Okay we need this much steel.'"

His records and his orders were behind. Thank goodness for Jack Chamberlain, the foreman for the guys who actually built the transformers. Jack would come in from the yard and say, "Ray, um, you'd better order some cold rolled steel."

"What are you talking about Jack?" Ray would answer. "We've got eighty yards here. You just can't find it."

Jack would smile. "Trust me Ray, order some."

"If it wasn't for him I would have been fired because I would have been out of material all the time," Scampy admits. Fortunately, they never had to shut down, and even more fortunately for Ray, the GE job paid the bills until the NHL came calling.

Some of his early vocational efforts continue to pay off today. "I did take bookkeeping, business, and typing classes when I was in school, and I could type like a bandit—seventy-five words a minute," Scampy says with a smile. "Now it's like riding a bike. When I'm on a computer, I dance across the keyboard. Man, I'm cruising."

⁓

Scampy often says he's been lucky, been at the right place at the right time. Based on his early career breaks, and on the fact he survived three decades in North America's bloodiest sport unscathed, maybe he's right. But what is luck? Some say it's simply preparation meeting opportunity. That would fit Scampy in general, but it would be bunkum, as it relates to his luckiest moment. His impeccable timing was never more evident than on the day in 1975 when he stumbled across one Maureen Flaherty at Pearson Airport. Very few men are prepared to find the perfect mate, nor are they lucky enough to find her. This was indeed a fortuitous encounter.

Maureen worked for the Liquor Control Board at the airport. Ray would stop in to purchase gifts and mementos while journeying around the continent. Gradually a friendship, lunches, and the like developed into romance, and in 1979 the couple married.

"Our first date, if you can call it that, was at a restaurant across from the airport because Ray had a late flight. I was constantly saying goodbye to him. We dated three or four years before we married," Maureen points out. "By that time, I had a pretty good idea about his business, the travel, and what the lifestyle entailed."

Maureen would rarely accompany Ray on the road. On occasion, however, because of the proximity to Toronto and Guelph, she'd make the car trip to Buffalo.

"I'd drop Maureen off at this Galleria Mall in Buffalo in the afternoon, go do the game, and then pick her up at a restaurant next to the mall after the game was over, about ten o'clock," Ray explains. "She'd be in shopping mode for eight hours with my credit card—scary.

"Anyway, ten years ago or so, I get to the rink in Buffalo and a fan tells me the game has been cancelled because the scoreboard had crashed to the ice. I'm like, 'Yeah, right.'" In fact, the scoreboard had crashed to the ice the morning of the game, fortunately when none of the players were skating.

"So I confirm the game is cancelled, and then I have to go and pick up Maureen," Ray continues. "I couldn't find her, and they wouldn't page her because I screwed up and told the mall guy it wasn't an emergency. I walked end to end in that damn mall for hours and never found her. We met at the restaurant at ten o'clock. Malls drive me crazy."

This will be a source of mockery for Scampy's cohorts, but there's a certain Ward and June Cleaver element to the Scapinellos. Okay, make that a certain June Cleaver element, thanks to an extremely nice, unselfish, and agreeable woman.

"Ray always made me feel my time at home was urgent for his success," Maureen points out, "and he meant it."

"Thank you for what you do. If you weren't here, I wouldn't be able to do my job," Ray often said.

"I always took great pride in knowing that I was helping him with what he does best. I never tried to distract him when he was on the road. It doesn't do any good to hammer him with stuff. To make this kind of profession work, you have to have strong people behind you at home," Maureen insists. Of course she's right, and of course there's nothing wrong this day and age, despite a modern cultural tendency to promote the opposite, with having a traditional breadwinner, supported by a traditional family.

~

Ray Scapinello is indeed a family man, first and foremost. In 1978, prior to meeting Maureen, Ray purchased a house in Guelph across the street from his parents. He still resides there today, living on the same street since he was fourteen years old.

Having strong family support is important simply because of the nature of officials' on-ice profession. It's high profile, and from the fans' perspective, it's usually high-profile negative. One difficult issue for officials that can affect family is that almost everyone hates them. The officials are anonymous for the most part, and during a game it's easy to assume that every person in the building despises the men in stripes. The fans cheer every time an official falls or gets hurt, and they boo almost every decision. Call this the ultimate "nature of the beast."

In 1984, when Ryan Scapinello was four years old, he was sitting with his mother in the end zone blues at Maple Leaf Gardens, watching his father, his hero, officiate a game. A player slapped the puck into the offensive zone along the boards, just as another player stepped in front of Ray and blocked his view. The puck rammed the linesman in the side of the head and down he went, to the delight of many in the crowd. Dad was hurt, but fans were laughing and cheering. This seemed a startling development for Ryan—the four-year-old's equivalent of "what the hell is going on?"

"It was evident from the look on my face that Ray was hurt, and I was concerned," Maureen remembers. "Yet the crowd was jeering. I felt sorry for Ryan. He didn't understand it, but it's like that for all of the officials' kids. It was his introduction to the mixed response for his father's profession. It's a tough lesson; some people take great delight in mocking and saying nasty things."

The trainers helped Ray off, and a few minutes later, much to the relief of his utterly confused young son in particular, he hopped back onto the ice, this time wearing a helmet as a precaution.

"It was tough finding a helmet to fit his cranium," Maureen says, "so it looked funny. Fortunately, that turned out to be the most traumatic part of it."

For his March 2004 beaning in Toronto, Maureen was watching the game at home on *Hockey Night in Canada*.

"At that point, I was pretty sure Ray would be just fine. When he got hit in the fanny, he jumped right back up, with Gary Bettman's signature tattooed to his rear. And when he got hit in the head, he was right by the door," Maureen recalls. "He went off, and came back out without a helmet. If he could skate with a broken leg, he'd do it."

Despite Scampy's apparent quick recovery, Maureen put on her coat and was waiting by the door when he came home.

"She was worried about my head, and she wanted to take me to hospital in Guelph. I explained to her that I had just seen five of the best doctors," Scampy says. He convinced her they should stay home.

~

Strangely enough, it was Scampy's early baseball abilities—he was a talented left-handed shortstop—that led to his career in hockey officiating.

"A gentleman who later became [NHL referee] Bill McCreary's father-in-law, Mel McPhee, knew me from playing baseball," Scampy says. "He was a member of the Guelph Referees Association, and asked me if I'd be interested in joining, to stay in hockey. I thought that was a really good idea.

Scampy joined the Guelph Referees Association (G.R.A.) while he was handling the transformer gig at Canadian GE. He started out by working children's hockey, three or four games in a row each Saturday morning. Obviously, at that point, the NHL was the furthest thing from his mind. Once he had a bit of experience, he made a tactical decision to increase his cash flow.

"There were three or four guys who were G.R.A. members who were a lot older than me, who jumped over and ref'ed in this local, 'outlaw' junior-A league," Scampy recalls. "It had no affiliation with the Ontario Hockey Association (OHA), and was a complete rival. I followed them, and I got $7.50 a game—pretty damn good for being a linesman back in the late 1960s."

An OHA official warned him, "You'll never get in the OHA if you do *that* league."

"I don't care," Scampy answered. "I'm making much more here. I'm happy where I am."

The next year, 1970, Scampy earned an invitation to an NHL rookie officials' camp on the recommendation of Hall-of-Fame referee Frank Udvari. Udvari didn't know

Scampy; he invited the young Guelphite purely because of Ray's work on the ice. Scotty Morrison, the NHL's Referee-in-Chief under Clarence Campbell (later, named Vice President of Officiating, an officer of the League, under John Ziegler), ran the camp and invited about twenty to twenty-five young hopefuls.

"Frank Udvari gave me my break. He went to bat for me. He had Scotty Morrison's ear," Scampy reflects. "He was a supervisor who told Morrison to keep his eye on me. He was a Kitchener guy, well respected by coaches and GMs in the NHL. I remember he got Ron Wicks hired; Ron had worked for him way back in the OHA."

From the rookie camp, five guys were invited up to the regular NHL training camp. The criterion was simple: a combination of judgment, maturity, skating ability, enthusiasm, and knowledge of the game.

Scampy didn't make the cut.

"So, I went back to the outlaw league and minor hockey," Scampy explains. "Then, the OHA found out that I went to this camp, and there was a finder's fee if an official went on to the NHL, maybe about $2,000 or $3,000, so the OHA urged me to join. I picked up an application and joined."

Scampy worked the OHA for one season, then went back to the NHL rookie camp, this time selected as one of five called to the next level. At the NHL camp, Scampy made the grade. He was hired at age twenty-four, in 1971.

"At first, I thought I'd have to go to the Central League and get some seasoning," Scampy recalls. "That was the main feeder minor league at the time. But I lucked out.

Another Guelphite, George Ashley, a long-time NHL linesman, decided to retire that year, opening a spot in the big league, and I was chosen."

"Ray had talent," proclaims Morrison. "Obviously, the first thing was his outstanding skating ability. Also, his approach to officiating got him hired—his desire to do it to the best of his ability, his enthusiasm."

In his very early days, Ray's only problem seemed to stem from not wanting to follow all of the off-ice details.

"At that time," Morrison continues, "I had a firm policy: When you were traveling with the NHL, or on NHL business, particularly day of game, it was shirt and tie. Scampy used to love, if he thought I or Frank weren't going to be around, to put on that turtleneck. When we'd show up, the collars would go up on the overcoats."

"If I ever catch you wearing that turtleneck again, you'll be looking for another job," Morrison threatened early on. Scampy and the others quickly fell in line, while Morrison did what he could to keep the message across.

"Referee Wally Harris was an impeccable dresser," Morrison remembers. "Once, I walked into the dressing room and Harris was standing there with Scampy and another linesman. Harris had on dark pants and leather jacket, white shirt, and a tie underneath."

"I'm surprised," Morrison uttered. "It's a gorgeous jacket, Wally, but wouldn't that really look a lot nicer with a turtleneck sweater?"

~

CHAPTER 4

Over a one- or two-year period, Morrison hired three pretty short linesmen: Ray, Claude Bechard, and Willie Norris. Clarence Campbell wasn't a big joker, but he did like to tease Morrison about hiring the "midgets."

"I thought you were hiring them based on the fact you could talk to them eyeball to eyeball," Campbell would tell Morrison.

"They may be small, but they don't hesitate to jump into altercations," Morrison would answer after a laugh.

"Not afraid of anything," Morrison repeats now, "and Ray has a rapport like no other."

"The rapport comes from experience," Scampy states. "I've always gotten along pretty well with people, communicated pretty well, but combined with being on the ice and dealing with players, it just kind of evolved naturally for me."

Scampy also credits his more experienced predecessors for showing him the way.

"I learned a lot from John D'Amico and Matt Pavelich," Scampy stresses. "John was my mentor when I started in the business, and in my opinion, he was the best linesman I ever saw in my thirty-three years. He was so in tune and aware of what was going on on the ice at all times. He knew exactly who was angry with someone for something that happened earlier in the game, and he always knew when guys were coming out of the penalty box. Now, we're supposed to be there to escort a guy out of the box; we're supposed to know at 12:14 of the second period a guy is coming out. Even on the fly, you've got to keep an eye on anything that might occur with a guy coming out. D'Amico was in tune with that stuff long before it was in vogue or part of the protocol."

Scampy remembers working a game in Detroit in the early seventies when Matt Pavelich missed an offside by a couple feet. No one said a word.

"I was back at the red line watching and wondering what the hell was going on," Scampy remembers. "No one ever said a word or questioned him on it, eh? The respect he had ... John D'Amico and Matt Pavelich had unbelievable respect."

Scampy wondered if that day would ever come for him; when *he'd* get that kind of respect. He's proved that much of it comes with experience.

"Me," Scampy jokes, "they're usually on me like a cheap suit, usually telling me to get my head out of my ass. Get your head out of your ass!"

Right up through Ray's retirement and even after, three or four times a year, someone would come up to Ray and say, "Hi, Mr. D'Amico."

Ray would answer, "Hi, how are you? But my name is Ray Scapinello."

"Oh yeah, sorry Ray."

John D'Amico. Also an Italian guy. Also no hair.

"But what a tribute to John," Scampy reasons. "He was off the ice for fifteen years or so, and people still thought of him and his name."

In the summer of 2005, D'Amico passed away in Toronto after a long illness.

"I talked to his son, Angelo, and his wife, Dorothy, on occasion to see how he was doing after we found out he was sick," Scampy explains. "One day in the summer, I asked Dorothy how he was doing and she said, 'Not good.' I offered to come see him the next day and she said, 'You'd better come down today.'"

Ray showered, jumped in his truck, and was at the hospital in an hour and a half.

"We reminisced, we talked a little hockey, and then I gave him a hug before I left," Scampy recalls. "A couple of days later he passed."

When Scampy enters the Hall of Fame, maybe people will stop mixing him up with D'Amico. Scampy wouldn't mind a bit if they didn't.

"I consider John a friend and a mentor and he's missed dearly by his friends in the hockey world," Ray concludes. "It was an honor to learn from him."

~

Considering the personal historical tie-in, it comes as no surprise that Scampy never lost his appreciation for baseball, and his love of the diamond.

During his early days in the NHL, he played softball for his brother's team, Rags For Men, named after Dougie's clothing store in Kitchener. Scampy yapped on the ballfield as if he was on the ice, goading players on the opposition, and waving at fans who booed or yelled at him. It was a very competitive men's senior softball league, an industrial league, and Rags For Men had the reputation of buying the best team available.

"People always thought we were stocking ringers, because we were always pretty damn good," Scampy remembers. "But we always got our ass kicked in the finals. We never won a championship. We'd have a wonderful regular schedule and early playoffs, and then get to the finals and get our asses kicked."

A team from Sprucedale, just outside of Guelph, made up of farm kids would always beat Scampy's team in the end.

"Out in the field, bringing in the friggin' hay all day, they'd show up in their blue jeans and work shirts and kick our ass every time," Scampy recalls. "We had the nice softball pants, jerseys, and hats. Big deal. Balls would go over our heads into the cornfield one after another.

"They went about their business, never trash-talked, never complained or argued with the umpires," he points out. "If a guy was called out on a bad call, the kid would get up, dust himself off, come up again, and hit the ball out of the park."

This was surely a perfect example of substance over style, and another life lesson for Ray. More substance for George Scapinello's son: Work hard, stay humble, be the best.

Gaining Experience

They're good officials and they're going to be around a long time.
—Referee-in-Chief Scotty Morrison, responding to NHL
President Clarence Campbell, autumn 1971

"My whole goal was to be considered one of the best linesmen to lace up a pair of skates," Ray Scapinello says. Mission accomplished, although it didn't come without growing pains.

His first-ever NHL game took place in Buffalo, with the Sabres hosting the North Stars on October 17, 1971. Apparently it was so uneventful that Scampy doesn't even remember it, or maybe he was so nervous that he blacked out the evening. For the record, Detroit native Charlie Burns scored two of the eleven goals he'd net that season, including the game winner, in Minnesota's 3–2 victory. The referee was Ron Wicks and Scampy's partner on the lines was Willy Norris.

"I have no recollection of that evening—not even showing up at the rink," Scampy insists.

Two months later, on December 15, Buffalo traveled to Chicago to take on the Blackhawks in a game he'll *never* forget. It was Wednesday night and Chicago Stadium was a madhouse as usual. Scampy had hair back then, and the ones on the back of his neck were standing up as he listened to the national anthem, or rather the deafening screams, applause, and cheers that drowned out the actual song. Bobby Hull and Stan Mikita started skating around; Tony Esposito was in net.

"I loved Chicago Stadium," Scampy declares. "The organ, the fans, the anthem. Oh my God, if you couldn't get up for a game there, you must have been dead. It was impressive, the noisiest [rink] by far."

Bobby Hull took a feed from Pit Martin and rifled one past Buffalo goaltender Dave Dryden to make it 1–0 just four minutes into the game. Despite the early tally, coach Punch Imlach's Sabres managed to keep it close against the powerful Blackhawks, and stayed down just the one goal well into the second period.

Late in the second, the Sabres were putting pressure on the home team when rookie linesman Ray Scapinello made a costly blunder. Buffalo had the puck, moving down the ice, "minding their own business" as Scampy puts it, when they tried to dump the puck deep in the Chicago zone and get a line change. Behind the play a Buffalo defenseman tried to hurry off the ice. His replacement hopped on. The puck was knocked down at the Chicago blue line and a quick transition ensued. Chicago started right back up the ice. Realizing the dump wasn't successful, the defenseman who was headed off did a quick U-turn and stayed on the ice. The guy who had jumped over the boards to come on quickly jumped back off. No problem.

"Early first season, being as dumb as a rock," Scampy says seriously, "I call 'too many men on the ice.'"

Scampy blew his whistle. The players appeared a bit confused and coasted around wondering why play had been stopped. Scampy delivered the news, and it was not good for Buffalo.

"Punch Imlach was so livid, he refused to put a guy in the box," Scampy explains. "He was *that* angry."

After a reasonable delay, referee Art Skov confronted Punch.

"Punch, you have to put a guy in the box," Skov told him.

"Nope. No way," Punch answered. "I'm not putting a guy in the box for that call." In so many words, he expressed feelings that it was the worst call he'd seen in his life. Imlach continued to refuse and Skov put the watch on him. It took another full minute, with the referee ready to bang Buffalo for delay-of-game, before Imlach came to his senses and sent Phil Goyette into the penalty box.

The call came at 14:34 of the second period. One minute and one second later, on a long feed from goalie Esposito, Hull sped up the boards and ripped another past Dryden for a power play goal and a 2–0 lead.

On the official Penalty Record from NHL Game #208, penalty keeper Joe Rys wrote across the line: Goyette/T. Many Men/14:34//10//R-15:35/by Linesman Sapinello.

The slip of the pen and spelling faux pas was exceeded only by the headline in the *Chicago Tribune* sports section the next morning, which said "Scapinello, Hull Beat Sabres 2–1." There was a quote from Punch Imlach saying, "I don't know who this kid is, but one number higher and he'd be out of the league."

Punch was referring to an official's jersey number, which reflects his pecking order based on seniority; for example, the referees may be numbers 2 to 12, and the linesmen may be 13 to 33. Ray had a high number, thus Punch's reference to Ray's number.

(By the way, Scampy had a bunch of different numbers over the years. He was probably number 32 his first year. He also wore number 36 and number 42 along the way. He finished with 53 because he didn't care what number he wore. He had no superstitious reasons for having a number, nor did any number bring him luck. Scampy ended up with 53 when Dave Baker, who worked in the officials' office, asked Scampy to give up his lower number a few years ago because the referees at the time needed it.)

Scampy was dying inside. The next day he flew out to San Francisco to do a Seals game.

"I'm traveling with Neil Armstrong, a future Hall-of-Famer, and I'm a nervous wreck," Scampy remembers. "I'm thinking when I land in San Francisco, there's going to be a message: 'Hey stupid, go on home, you're done,' from Scotty Morrison."

So a fidgety Ray Scapinello sat on the plane with Armstrong, yearning for a little moral support. Scampy was hoping the veteran official would build him up, help give him back his confidence, tell him that things would be fine.

"Mr. Armstrong," Scampy said, "what'd you think of the call? That 'too many men on the ice'—what'd you think?"

In his high-pitched, squeaky voice while twisting his hair, Armstrong answered, "I wouldn't have called it."

Scampy went blank. Hmmm. Then he thought to himself, "Thanks for the vote of confidence, Neeeeiiilll." Then he went back to thinking about being in hot water.

∼

Obviously, like in any line of work, improvement for a linesman naturally comes with experience. Unfortunately, more is usually learned from the tough experiences.

Very early in his career, Scampy was taking a ton of heat from then Buffalo Sabres forward Eddie Shack about a call. Shack was just drilling him, and Scampy basically froze. It developed into ridiculous verbal abuse. Veteran referee Bob Myers came flying over from nowhere and banged Shack with a ten-minute misconduct. It was a call Scampy could have made himself.

"The referee had to come over and baby-sit me," Scampy recalls. "Myers was thinking, if you're not going to do anything about it, I am. Shack was berating me and I didn't stand up for myself."

It was early in Scampy's career and it was a valuable learning experience. He vowed right then and there never to put up with abuse.

"You've got a job to do. Do it," Scampy reiterates.

Missed calls will happen. Being in good physical condition, being focused and alert, and being in the right place all contribute to preventing missed calls. As confidence grows for a linesman, the likelihood of a missed call decreases even more.

Retired veteran linesman Wayne Bonney remembers being in an absolute funk for an opening round playoff game in Boston. It was Game Two, Edmonton/Boston, on May 18, 1990, and Scampy was actually the backup.

"There was always an extra referee for a playoff game," Scampy points out. "That was the one referee system. You didn't want three linesmen on the ice. Occasionally you'd have an extra linesman waiting also. As the rounds moved on, they definitely had both. You'd replace a guy if he was hurt, but you'd never replace him during a game for alleged poor performance. You live and die with the assignment."

"I was working a game at the Garden with Jay Shearers and Don Koharski," Bonney says. "My first period of my first playoff game that year and I was just brutal. I don't know if the boss up top knows it, but I know on the ice [when] I'm making mistakes."

Bonney needed help.

"I say to Jay Shearers, 'If you see anything close on my line, call it.'"

Bonney had lost confidence for whatever reason and couldn't get it back for the first twenty minutes of the game. It may have simply been the transition from the regular season into the pressure of the playoffs.

"It all came back in the second period. I was fine the rest of the way," Bonney recalls. "I don't know what it was in the first. I was horseshit. Koho and Jaybird stayed with me. I just blew a few calls and had a bad period."

Sometimes when it goes bad, there's no stopping it. Or as Bonney puts it, "You drop the puck and it hits everything on its way down to the ice, and God forbid you screw up and it ends up in the net."

While former Leafs right wing Rick Vaive scored fifty-plus goals for Toronto in three consecutive seasons—1982, 1983, and 1984, Bonney says one of those magic fifties shouldn't have counted.

"His fiftieth goal one season, I missed the offside call by a foot," Bonney admits. "The replay confirmed it. What can I say?"

~

"It's an impossible job done by some guys attempting to do the impossible," claims Toronto play-by-play man Joe Bowen. "It's probably the worst game of any professional sport to be an official [for]. A lot of us are overly critical of them because of how much of an impact they have on the game. A basketball official can call five hundred fouls, and it doesn't have an impact because both teams are shooting foul shots, but one penalty at a crucial time of a hockey game and it might decide it. I think they take an awful lot of abuse, but until you're down on the ice, a part of something that's moving at breakneck speed, you don't have an appreciation for it. As opposed to sitting up in the press box where we have a lot larger focus and a lot more time to see things ... it is pretty impossible to be overly critical, but we are anyway—fans are, parents are, and everyone else."

Even with the difficulty factor and his empathy for the zebras, there is one call after all these years that still bugs Bowen.

"I'm still a little bitter about the non-call on Gretzky in '93 that went on, but there are two sets of rules, and unfortunately in a situation like that, human nature takes part of it," Bowen points out.

What Bowen means by two sets of rules is that there was a very flexible set of rules that governed Gretzky, and a second set that applied to everyone else. In the NBA it would have been referred to as the Michael Jordan effect.

He goes on to explain that in Game Six of the conference finals, with the Maple Leafs leading the Kings three games to two, Wayne Gretzky high-sticked and sliced Toronto's Doug Gilmour in overtime but referee Kerry Fraser didn't call a penalty. Gilmour went for stitches, Gretzky scored the game winner, and LA went on to win the series in seven games.

"How do you throw the game's best player out?" Bowen continues, "But that was the cut-and-dry rule; if he draws blood, he's gone. That rule changed literally the next year to give them more leeway to make a call, whether it was two, four, or a game. As I say, instances like that can cost a team a game, and a chance to go to a Stanley Cup Final."

That story reinforces many things, among them that the pressure faced by a referee or a linesman can be unbelievable, and that the occupation is thankless. Often times, officials realize they're in a no-win situation even if they're doing an excellent job. Hometown fans, in particular, can be myopic.

"The most boisterous and rowdy were the Chicago fans back in the era of the old stadium," Scampy remembers.

"A lot of beer was consumed in that building and a lot of it came onto the ice. They didn't put up with much."

"I remember a game in Grand Rapids in the IHL ... I was working with a linesman from Detroit named Rick Welden," says veteran NHL linesman Mark Pare. "The home team was losing the game, a game they needed to win to set a record for most wins and ties at home ... they had gone unbeaten. The place was crowded and rowdy, it was 1978 I believe, and I think they were playing Fort Wayne. At one point, Grand Rapids had a chance to tie the game on a scramble. The goalie was reaching for the puck. The ref, Todd Larson, lost sight of it and blew the play dead, just as a Grand Rapids player found the puck and flipped it in. Todd had no choice but to wave it off because he'd blown the whistle. The place went nuts. A couple of players were ejected because they were so upset; I mean, these people really wanted to keep the perfect record at home. By the end of the game, I was worried about how we were going to get out of the arena, but when we showed up in the officials' room, there were ten cops wearing riot gear and helmets ready to escort us out. That was a comforting sight. We got two cruisers to escort us out to the highway so we could get out of harm's way."

"I had to run out of a building once, and I wasn't even a linesman anymore," states Ron Foyt. "After I'd retired, I became a video goal judge. I was working at the Met in Minneapolis for a North Stars/Islanders playoff game in overtime. Wally Harris was the supervisor next to me in the booth. A New York guy shot the puck so hard [that] it went in, it went out, and it went so fast they didn't see it. So, they sent it upstairs, and we ruled it a goal. It ended the North Stars season; in fact, I think it was the last game ever for the North Stars. The top row of the stands was right below the press box, and the fans started throwing beer at us. Season over, and we're getting pelted."

～

When questionable calls start to build up, at least in the minds of a local constituency, conspiracy theories are the next step. Many fans and members of the media in Toronto will sometimes claim the Maple Leafs are judged too harshly or that the League is out to get them, maybe because the NHL's officials' offices are in Toronto and thus the League goes over the top to avoid any Toronto favoritism.

"If you went to New York, or Montreal, there's probably conspiracy theories there as well," points out Bowen, "because there's so much media there. Especially in Toronto and Montreal, every call, every theory gets more attention because it's the center of the hockey universe, because of the size and the attention given the game. We have juniors, minors, pros. I don't think that the officials have that bias, or anti-bias."

One must also remember that in recent years in Toronto, the home team simply isn't that popular with the officials on a more personal level.

"I don't know if this has been true forever, but recently, the Leafs are very tough on the officials," points out Bowen's broadcast partner and former NHL coach Harry

Neale. "Quinn and the players yap a lot; they're probably the mouthiest team in the league. It incites the refs, and bad calls might be a reflection."

"Darcy Tucker agitates everyone," points out linesman Mark Pare. "He has as much interest in our job as he does his."

In the 2002 playoffs, Ottawa's Daniel Alfredsson cross-checked Tucker from behind into the boards, turned around, and scored a game winner at the Air Canada Centre. Referees Stephen Walkom and Rob Shick were criticized in Toronto for the non-call.

"You have a split second to decide," says Walkom. "On that particular call, you judge whether the player hit someone clean or not. I didn't have time to see whether it was Darcy. You don't have time to judge personality—you judge the act immediately, and you react immediately. Any time you delay, chances are you'll make the wrong call; think, and you'll screw it up."

"The officials had a meeting about that one and reviewed it," says ref Paul Devorski. "Aside from the fact I think they made the right decision, it's tougher because Darcy Tucker has built a reputation for diving. We see Tucker a lot. He'll writhe around; he's grabbing his face; he's rolling around. Officials can get tired of that sort of thing. We're gonna make sure it's a penalty before we call something."

Most of these "meetings" Devo refers to are virtual get-togethers. Every game is monitored by the NHL officials' staff in Toronto, in a room full of video monitors called "the war room." Some of the officials jokingly call it "mission control." The television feed of every game—exhibition, regular season, and playoffs—is monitored by the staff in the war room. If there's a goonish act that requires supplemental discipline, the war room gets the process started by marking the clip. Similarly, if there's a controversial call in a playoff game, the hockey operations staff will pull a clip, and then e-mail it out to all of the crews. If it's a big enough call, or one that hockey operations feels needs to be discussed, the supervisor overseeing each playoff series will review the play and discuss it with the refs and linesmen.

"It's an unbelievable learning tool," Scampy points out. "It was never intended to embarrass anyone. Everyone eventually gets sent good clips and bad clips. It wasn't intended to make a guy look bad, it was intended as a learning tool, and you get feedback almost immediately via e-mail. For a linesman, if he starts to drift out of position a lot, or has weak standards of puck drops or something, he'll get a clip."

The clips are also sent out to reinforce good calls and positive procedures during the regular season and the playoffs.

Prior to the new millennium, controversial calls were reviewed in person with a supervisor, or via conference call with many or all of the officials.

The idea is to seek constant improvement and consistency around the league, and to give no credence to conspiracy theories. Of course, no referee and linesman will ever be perfect … just ask the coaches.

"Pat Quinn is in a large club of guys behind the bench who mouth off a lot," adds Joe Bowen, "but he gets a lot of notoriety because he's in Toronto. Of course, when he talked to Scampy, he usually was responding to Scampy asking for gifts."

The mood lightens quickly when Bowen and Neale discuss Scapinello, who they tagged in recent years with the nickname "veal scaloppini" around his Italian roots.

"Anything silly involving Scampy, we'd replay it and have some fun," Neale points out.

"It's gonna be disappointing without Scampy around," Bowen continues. "He added a lot to it, which is amazing for a linesman. The players had a lot of respect for him. It's fun. You go back and watch the *Leafs TV* classic games, you see this little "veal scaloppini" parading around with dark hair, then thinning hair, and then no hair. His longevity, and then right 'til the end, to be regarded at the top of his game among the top three or four, at his advancing years, is a testament to his conditioning, his love of this game, and his tenacity," Bowen concludes.

"I can't believe he did all those games without missing one," Neale marvels, "breaking up guys twice his size and weight. If you're good enough to be one of the best, why retire?"

If it seems Neale has a certain affinity for the officials, a certain empathy for their trials and tribulations that come across on the air at times, it's understandable— Neale used to be one, albeit briefly, at a pretty high level.

∼

In 1966, Neale was hired as the second varsity hockey coach in Ohio State University history, following Glen Sonmor who moved on to the University of Minnesota.

"We had five scholarships, not good enough to compete with Michigan on a regular basis or anything, but we got a little better each of the four years I was there," the coach recalls. "I also taught a beginning hockey and skating class. I had [football players] Jack Tatum and Bruce Jankowski in the class, and I was terrified they might get hurt. Coach Woody Hayes was an aloof dictator; he wasn't a very friendly guy, and I wasn't about to tick off Woody."

About the same time Neale started the job, Columbus started up an IHL franchise.

"The International League in those days, they wanted local linesmen. They couldn't afford to travel them, and I was the only one around who had any hockey knowledge."

"You're the only guy who knows the pro rules," urged Frank Gallagher, GM of the Columbus Checkers.

"I don't even have a sweater or black pants. I've never even done a scrimmage," Neale protested.

Neale gave in, and for fifteen bucks a night, he lined in the IHL for one season and part of another when his schedule allowed.

"I was little, like Scampy, only with hair. I met [NHL ref] Dave Newell when he was a trainee, when he was in the IHL," Neale points out. "It gave me a real appreciation for the job. You can't win. Bad calls happen, and the coaches only remember the ones that go against them. You'd have a coach wanting to kill you, threatening you, over a missed offside call. Disputed goals were the worst, way before video review, of course. All coaches and players should referee at some point, anywhere, any level. They'd be more tolerant."

Neale eventually did road games, and traveled around the league, during the playoffs. His last ever game in 1968 involved Muskegon visiting Dayton in the finals.

"I remember George Burke and I were the linesmen, and we had a Central League ref. At the end of a period, we had to walk about twenty-five yards to the dressing room, with the fans right there," Neale recalls. "This one fan was walking along with the ref, literally screaming in his ear the whole way along. When we got to our door, having witnessed enough, I grabbed the guy by the lapels."

"If you've got something to say to us, come in the room and say it," Neale challenged. Later, he found out the guy was the president and GM of Muskegon. Enough was enough.

Neale wasn't about to risk his neck, and his career, over his part-time officiating job.

"They had some lunatics in the IHL. I remember during a brawl, I'm yelling to the ref and players, 'I'm not coming in, I'm not coming in!' I wasn't jumping in to get the shit kicked out of me."

~

Actual physical confrontation or contact between a coach or player and an official is rare in professional hockey, especially in the NHL. When it does occur, it's serious business.

Scampy was part of one the NHL's most famous and controversial confrontations, although the physical nature or degree of the incident remains in question. On May 6, following Game Three of the 1988 Wales Conference Finals, a 6–1 victory for Boston, New Jersey coach Jim Schoenfeld, upset over a series of penalties called against his team, confronted referee Don Koharski.

The officials had to exit the ice between the players' benches. The linesmen saw Schoenfeld waiting for them, and thought about delaying their exit.

"We don't have to wait for anyone," Koharski declared.

"After the teams went off the ice, we were coming off, and Schoenfeld blocked the walkway," Scampy remembers. "He confronted Koho, and after a few expletives, he supposedly bumped Don, who tumbled. When Koho righted himself, Schoenfeld said, 'You fell, you fat pig. Have another donut.' Don had either been bumped or stumbled over the edge of the mat, but at the time, I decided it was best to restrain Schoenfeld."

The League suspended Schoenfeld for the next game, which drew relief and praise from the officials. However, the suspension was short-lived. The Devils declared that during the day off, they had gotten a court injunction to allow Schoenfeld to coach the next game. The officials didn't find out about the legal reinstatement until just before Game Four.

"We had our pre-game meal and went to the rink," Scampy recalls. "We began stretching in the officials' room when [Director of Officiating] John McCauley came in and told us Schoenfeld would be behind the bench."

"What!?" came the reaction en masse.

"We're not working," referee Dave Newell said.

"Dave, you gotta work," McCauley told him.

"I'm not working," Newell insisted.

So McCauley turned to linesman Gord Broseker.

"Gordie, will you referee?"

"No, not if Dave's not going," Broseker responded.

McCauley turned to Scampy.

"Ray, will you ref?"

"John, if I go out and referee this game, I might as well go back to the hotel and jump off the roof," Scampy explained. "I work with these guys; I'm not going out on the ice."

Dennis Morel was the standby referee and he also refused to go out.

McCauley went to the New Jersey management and hoped they would understand the officials' stance. He suggested the assistant coaches run the team for the night. No such luck. New Jersey insisted they wanted Schoenfeld to coach.

McCauley went back to the officials' room and informed his men of the decision.

"I remember at one point when John had the door open, I saw what looked like a replacement official walk by in a yellow jersey," Scampy says.

McCauley's last words to the officials: "You guys know your contractual obligations." With that, McCauley slammed the door.

"We're fired," Scampy said to the guys. "And what a way to leave the business," he thought to himself. "This is awful."

Maureen Scapinello was preparing to watch the game at home.

"The TV coverage had started, but the lights in the rink weren't all the way up," Maureen remembers. "And then I hear, 'we're waiting for the arrival of the replacement officials.' What? All kinds of things were running through my head, like a van accident or something."

A few minutes later the phone rang. Scampy was on the other end.

"Everyone's fine, but I think we've been fired," Scampy told his wife.

"This was on Mother's Day," Maureen laughs. "It was not the phone call I had expected."

"Maureen, if I were to go out there, I might as well go back to the hotel roof and jump. We have to be unified."

"All night long I'm thinking it was fun while it lasted," Maureen recalls. "I started thinking about Ray working at General Electric again. Not a minute of sleep that night."

Phil Shulman, aka "Flip" and Ray's long-time friend in New York, attended the game.

"The players came out to warm-up, a girl came out to sing the anthem, and then she didn't sing—she walked off," Flip remembers. "Hey, where's Scampy? Where are the officials?" Flip wondered, as he began to worry.

"Above and beyond, the biggest dilemma was the fact that our guys loved John McCauley," Scampy points out. "He was a great guy and boss, and this was the last thing we wanted to do to him and put him through."

At one point McCauley's wife said to the officials, "I can't believe you did that to John."

CHAPTER 5

"That was tough, but we did what we had to do," Scampy resolves. "If it wasn't for Dave Newell, we probably would have gone out. There's a good chance no one else would have had the intestinal fortitude to do what Newell had done. He thought a grave injustice had been done, and we showed solidarity and backed him up."

The replacement officials made it through the game. It came off without a major hitch, and nobody was injured. The game was officiated by off-ice officials—Paul McInnis, Jim Sullivan, and Vin Godleski—timekeepers, goal judges, and such who were pulled out of the stands and they went out and got the job done.

"We didn't really have the right to do what we did, and we were glad nobody got hurt," Scampy points out. "But the funniest thing ever was the response Harry Sinden gave after the game."

When someone asked the Bruins' GM what he thought of the officiating, Harry said, "I didn't notice any difference." Particularly biting, considering the Bruins lost Game Four, 3–1.

The next day, John McCauley refused to ride in the cab with the NHL officials to the airport. Scampy and the crew flew to Toronto. When they arrived, a dozen NHL officials were waiting for them. The officials went to a meeting at the Holiday Inn. NHL President John Ziegler phoned the officials' attorney, Jim Beatty, and said, "The game will go on in Detroit tonight and after that we'll deal with the officials who refused to work."

Jim Beatty responded, "Try again. What happens to those four officials will determine whether or not there are NHL officials tonight in Detroit."

After a very tense hour or so, Ziegler phoned back and said there would be no retribution for the officials who took their stand. The Detroit game went on, and none of the officials who sat out the New Jersey game were fired. It didn't affect overall status either, as both Scampy and Newell went on to work the Finals that spring.

In retrospect, it had been broadcast that Schoenfeld had pushed Koharski. In reality, according to Scampy, Schoenfeld had blocked Koharski's path and Don stumbled off the edge of the carpet. They were at close quarters and it looked like Schoenfeld had bumped him. The concept of bumping the official, and the degree of the bump, could have, and probably would have, changed a lot of elements surrounding the controversy. Had Schoenfeld literally shoved the ref, or punched him, he would have been tossed for at least the rest of the playoffs. Instead, Schoenfeld ended up sitting out Game Five, which his team lost 7–1, and his Devils lost the series in seven games. (Lost in all of this: the series was fast-paced, furious, hard-hitting, and a lot of fun to watch.)

One of the worst examples of physical confrontation in NHL history actually involved a fan and a referee, and it wasn't an NHL match-up that triggered the violence.

In 1979, the Russians played against the NHL in a best-of-three Challenge Cup. The Russians made a strong statement by holding an edge in the series, including a final win at Madison Square Garden to win the Cup two games to one.

After the game, referee John McCauley went across the street from the arena for a drink with his linesmen. Cold war feelings obviously overwhelmed one drunken American, who resented the loss and apparently McCauley's performance in the game. The fan sucker-punched McCauley in the eye, knocked him silly, and inflicted an eye socket injury that eventually would end McCauley's career as an NHL ref. Two years later, after a long recovery and a brief comeback on the ice, he went to work for Scotty Morrison in the League office, overseeing the officials.

"John was always a good individual," Scampy reminisces. "He called a spade a spade. If you had an argument with him tonight, by tomorrow night it's a forgotten deal. He never held grudges. Generally, we really enjoyed working for him."

Scampy last saw McCauley following the last game of the Flames/Canadiens final, won by Calgary in Montreal in the spring of 1989, not long before McCauley died. The NHL held a post-game reception at the Sheraton. Scampy had a couple beers and was heading off to bed when McCauley, sitting with his son and daughter, motioned Scampy over to the table. The two recapped some of the moments of the series before Scampy called it a night.

"John, I want to thank you for giving me the Stanley Cup Finals this year."

"Scamp, you're a credit to the business."

With that, Ray walked off, never to speak to McCauley again. A couple of weeks later, McCauley died at age forty-four.

"I got a phone call and I was dumbfounded," Scampy recalls sadly.

Apparently McCauley ignored warning signs of an internal problem—liver or gallbladder—and by the time he considered taking action it was too late.

∼

The McCauley punching incident accentuates the difference between the job of a referee and the job of a lineman. As experienced and well-traveled as Scampy was, the pressure he was under at times paled in comparison to the pressure faced by a referee on a regular basis.

"On a scale, if a linesman's pressure is a 5, a referee's pressure is a 12," says Wayne Bonney. Bonney was a linesman for several years, and his two attempts to become a referee failed.

"I tried refereeing in the WHA for a couple years and it didn't work out. When I came to the National League in 1979, John McCauley said, 'Wayne, you can give refereeing a shot.'"

After seeing his first game, McCauley said to Bonney, "You know what you need?"

"What?" Bonney answered.

"You need to learn what a penalty is. You're not very good," McCauley told him.

Bonney had called everything—anything remotely resembling a penalty. The next game, Bonney overcompensated and called nothing. McCauley didn't mind this so much, because personally, he enjoyed letting the players play.

"Much better," he told Wayne. "One of the better games I've seen."

That was it, the tryout was over. It wasn't until the next season's training camp that Bonney raised the issue again.

"So, John, am I gonna get a shot at ref'ing again?"

"Oh, I thought we discussed that already," McCauley answered. "You're not refereeing."

Where linesmen might have something controversial once in a blue moon, referees are confronted with critical analyses night in and night out.

"Linesmen go year to year pretty confident that they're going to keep their jobs. Referees, a lot of them, worry about whether or not they're going to have a job year after year. It's completely different. If they screw up enough, they're done," Bonney points out. "Scampy and I, I don't think we ever really worried about our jobs. Refs have to worry every season."

"That's kind of a blanket statement by Wayne. I mean, if a linesman is consistently poor, he's going to be looking for new work as well," Scampy points out. "It's just there's a lot more controversy and such surrounding the refs. I never went to training camp assuming anything. I felt I'd have my job, but I never assumed I'd be working deep into the playoffs or anything. That's why I treated every game with the same importance."

Officials receive evaluations at the middle of the season. They can be called in, or contacted, if their performance is suffering at any time.

"You'll hear about it; you'll get a rating," Scampy says. "Not like a number, but you'll get a verbal evaluation. By the way, there's no question the referees have a lot more issues to cover, and a lot more potential problems to address."

Another by-product of the pressure differences between referees and linesmen is illustrated in their travel schedules. Mostly for cost reasons, linesmen stay within a region. Referees can't. Too many of their calls are too big, too many are remembered, and it would be unfair to a ref to let the ire of the fans, coaches, and players build up in a particular city or region.

"Unless I'm blowing offside calls that lead to goals all the time," Scampy points out, "there's a pretty good chance I can work in the same bunch of cities over and over and go unnoticed. A referee couldn't survive it. One bad call could turn a coaching staff on a guy for a long time. The refs move around a lot just so they don't have to keep seeing the same fans, coaches, and players. Their impact is too great to keep showing up in the same place."

Scampy remembers one of the occasions when he was forced to take on the extra responsibility because of an injury. Early in a game in Buffalo, ref Dave Newell got ran into, and Scampy was called upon to wear the orange stripe. To make sure the demands and expectations didn't get too high, Ray immediately skated up to Florida coach Mike Keenan and said, "I'll be refereeing now. You know I don't

know anything about ref'ing, and I know I don't know anything about ref'ing, so leave me alone." Keenan laughed
while Scampy skated away, and Keenan left him alone.

During the regular season, back-up referees are not
considered necessary or practical for financial reasons.
Plus, there are not enough referees to go around. Usually,
the senior linesman takes over in case of injury.

Speaking of back-ups, Wayne Bonney remembers a
refereeing maneuver that wouldn't be considered controversial, but rather savvy in a sneaky sort of way.

"During a playoff game in Quebec, the Canadiens
were playing against the Nordiques; it was Andy Van
Hellemond, Bob Hodges, and myself. Don Koharski was
the standby ref. Before the game, during the warm-up, the
teams had a big brawl. Koho comes down and says, 'Come
on guys, let's go. There's a big brawl out there.' Hodgy and
I start to get ready."

"Hold it," Van Hellemond advised.

"What?" Bonney questioned.

"Hear the cheering? When you hear the booing, that's
when we're going out. Take your time," Van Hellemond rea-
soned. So the two linesmen took their time, and sure enough,
the cheers turned to boos. The officials went out on the ice and
the fighters had gradually broken the fight up themselves.

"We went out. It was done. We didn't have to write a
report. Koharski wrote down all of the numbers from the
stands, and he was writing reports for three days," Bonney
adds. "Andy was very savvy; he had a lot of tricks."

~

As one might expect, pay reflects responsibility. In 2004, a new linesman made about $70,000 a year, while a new NHL ref made about $100,000. Long-time linesmen made something in the mid-$100,000s, while referees could earn almost double that. In the playoffs, linesmen made about $9,000 or $10,000 a round; referees made $12,000.

"That's what it's all about," adds Bonney. "Making the finals is prestige and money. What Scampy did—twenty of them—is unbelievable. I did three in a row, missed, then did two, and then never saw it again."

Bonney's last Final was Detroit against New Jersey in 1995. He retired in 2003. These days, he gets plenty of opportunities to empathize with young referees and linesmen; he's the Director of Officiating for the double-A Central Hockey League.

〜

One incident that defies the referee/linesman comparison involved linesman Ron Foyt the day before Halloween in 1983. Foyt had come over from the WHA, and was absorbed into the NHL staff in 1979 along with Ron Asselstine, Ron Fornier, and Bonney.

Tom Lysiak of the Blackhawks, upset over being waved out of a face-off by Foyt, slew-footed the linesman after he dropped the puck. Foyt went down hard backwards, but got right back up. Lysiak earned a game misconduct from referee Dave Newell, and also earned a twenty-game suspension, the first under a new abuse-of-officials rule. (Previously, Lysiak had apparently been involved in bumping incidents with Newell and Andy Van Hellemond.)

From there, politics took over. Lysiak was one of Chicago's best players, and during his suspension, the Blackhawks went into a funk. The suspension essentially ruined Chicago's season, and back in the day when the owners ruled in entirety, it's believed Chicago owner Bill Wirtz ordered John McCauley to release Foyt. Scampy remembers going to McCauley to protest, believing Foyt was a damn good official. McCauley said his hands were tied.

For the most part, on-ice contact between the players and officials is accidental.

"I've pirouetted my way out of the way more times than I can remember," Scampy laughs, "but we've all been bumped and bounced."

Joe Bowen remembers a humorous on-ice incident involving an official—an accidental, unavoidable collision.

"Dave 'Snapper' Newell one night, who I've known since I was a kid from Sudbury, was skating around the rink at Joe Louis Arena kind of minding his own business during a pre-game warm-up," Bowen tells it. "Detroit goalie Greg Stefan had this personal tradition where he'd run as fast as he could in his goalie gear out of the runway, and explode onto the ice at full speed. You could see from our vantage point that this was going to be one hell of a collision and neither one of them saw it coming. Out comes Stefan and bang, down goes Snapper, and he was unconscious," Bowen continues. "The game was delayed because Snapper couldn't press on. Eventually the Leafs poured about three or four past Stefan in the first period and went on to win the game. Of course, Stefan blamed Newell for it, for the collision, and for affecting his concentration," Bowen says with amazement. "I mean, what the hell, these guys can't win for losing.

"I've always loved Bill McCreary and those guys," Bowen concludes. "They're tremendous individuals, and they do a tremendous job, especially with all of the travel and everything. It's a wonder there aren't more problems."

Terry Gregson, who retired in the spring of 2004 with Scampy, wasn't so lucky with his on-ice collision. Any form of immediate recovery was out of the question.

"Back about January of 1989, I broke my collarbone. Was out about seven weeks," Gregson recalls. "In Montreal, I was skating up the boards, and Stephane Richer turned towards the boards and we collided. I wasn't prepared for that move. I had a bit of a concussion, to go with the collarbone."

Gregson also sat out twenty-eight days in 2003, after getting smooshed from behind by Stephane Quintal in Philadelphia. Gregson dislocated his shoulder when he hit the ice. As illustrated earlier, this is an area where the difference between referees and linesmen ends. The potential to get crushed exists for both.

~

Meanwhile, Mr. Scapinello avoided all of that. The closest he ever came to missing an assignment was due to a sketchy travel decision. He was scheduled to do a game in New York, leaving Toronto on a nine o'clock flight the morning of the game. Don Koharski, who was living near

Scampy in Burlington at the time, was also doing the game, so Scampy gave him a call.

"Koho, are you on the nine?"

"No, I'm taking the ten."

"Boy, that's a little late. We should be gone by nine," Scampy countered.

"I'm on the ten," Koharski insisted. "They're not calling for bad weather."

"Ok, well, I'll see you in New York." Scampy got off the phone, checked the weather again, and decided maybe an extra hour of sleep wouldn't be too bad. He switched to the ten o'clock flight.

Like clockwork, Scampy got up, drove to the airport, boarded the plane, and took off on time. While nearing New York, the plane circled for what seemed like an hour. They couldn't land the plane because of super-high winds, and instead of diverting to Philly or Boston or Hartford, they decided to return to Toronto. The plane landed back in Toronto at about 1:00 p.m.; the game in New York was at seven.

"I'm not calling Bryan Lewis. I'll quit first," Scampy told Koho. Scampy was beside himself.

Koho said, "I'll call him." Koharski explained the situation to Lewis without explaining the part about leaving on a ten o'clock flight when they should have left at nine.

"You guys get there," Lewis said, but he made contingencies anyway. Ron Hogarth was just about to leave Long Island after doing an Islanders game the night before and Lewis was able to catch him. Hogarth was on call.

Scampy and Koharski caught an afternoon flight to Philly, and then a puddle jumper to Islip Airport out on

Long Island. They drove like banshees, and arrived seven or eight minutes into the first period. Scampy changed on the fly with Richard Trottier; they gave each other a high five as they made the switch. Meanwhile, Lewis wouldn't let Koharski work. There would be no change of referees midstream.

The next day Scampy was doing a game in Hartford when he ran into Bryan Lewis at the rink and said hello. Lewis handed him an envelope with a letter. It was a reprimand for not traveling within League policy and included a fine for $250. It was the first and last time Scampy broke travel regulations.

"I'd like to blame Koho but I couldn't. It was my decision to change flights," Scampy resolves.

Maybe it was the incident involving getting to New York that did it, but as his career went on, Scapinello became obsessive about getting to games early.

"I remember too many times arriving in a snowstorm when you couldn't believe you were arriving," Scampy reasons. Scampy drove to most games in his region—Detroit, Buffalo, Montreal, and Pittsburgh, for example. If the weather might be tough, he'd arrive ten hours ahead of the puck drop, rather than two or three.

In the early days, problems with driving occurred for completely different reasons ... mainly that Ray didn't know how to take care of his car.

"One time, I had to roll my car down the hill by my house and push it into the gas station," Ray remembers. "And I had to get to the airport." Enter Bill Rowley.

"I was in the insurance salvage business and owned a wrecking yard in Guelph in the 1970s," Rowley recalls. "I get this call one day from a service station owner. He was holding the phone in one hand, and the carburetor from Scampy's car in the other."

"I can't fix this thing," the man said. "We need a new carburetor."

"Well, I had four thousand cars on the yard," Rowley continues, "so I found the part I thought would fit, and brought it on over. We worked on it, Scampy's car started, and away he went."

It's not surprising that with so many people in Scampy's life, a chance meeting turned into a lifetime friendship. Over the years, Scampy took Bill to games in Buffalo, Detroit, and Montreal. They still skate together on occasion in Guelph, and their families spend time together during the summer.

Another friend and associate, current NHL linesman Brad Kovachik, who resides near Scampy in Ontario, has followed the veteran's lead by driving often and by getting to destinations early.

"I've been lucky as it relates to travel," Kovachik says. "I'm a driver, too. I prefer driving if I can. Like Ray once said, 'Good thing about driving ... every time the wheels turn, you're that much closer to home.'"

For the most part, linesmen work two to three games a week. If they end up working two weekends in a row, they'll get the third weekend off.

"Nowadays I might be gone for ten days, max," Scampy says. "In the old days—holy cow—we'd be gone for three weeks at a time. There were less of us, and we were all over the place. The regional setup is a lot better, although during the playoffs you can end up anywhere in the country. Playoffs are all-important; the money is not the issue."

In his last few seasons, Scampy basically stuck to games east of Chicago. This reality, and the location of Scampy's home, may have a lot to do with his notoriety. Based near Toronto, the unofficial center of the hockey universe, Scampy believes the regional setup to his job assignments has allowed him to reap exposure.

"A lot of guys have done my job but don't have the reputation," Scampy says. "I think I've benefited from being near Toronto. This area is a bit more of a high-profile situation than, say, Randy Mitton working in Edmonton, or somebody in Calgary, or somebody working in LA—not that they're not good linesmen. They just might not get the notoriety that someone gets around here."

Southern Ontario seems to be a hotbed for officials who move up to hockey's highest level, with countless representatives in the NHL from areas west and southwest of Toronto. Part of it may be the OHA's reputation for developing high-quality officials. As the years pass, that reputation develops legacies.

"Our dad, Bill, was a referee in the OHA for thirty-five years," points out NHL ref Paul Devorski, referring to himself and NHL linesman brother Greg. "I actually did the lines for my dad when he was still working."

Devo played junior and senior hockey in Ontario, but tired of the bus trips. His best opportunity to stay involved in the game came via his father's profession. He went from the OHA to the OHL to the NHL without ever having to work a minor league game.

NHL ref Bill McCreary came from a similar background.

"I played junior hockey in the early 1970s, and I wasn't very good. The OHL was the end of it for me," McCreary recalls. "I first officiated little kids in Guelph, to give something back to the community, then the OHA, which at that point included major junior under one umbrella. I spent one year on the lines, and one year refereeing. Scotty Morrison invited me to NHL camp as a ref."

NHL linesman Mark Pare also began his career officiating children as a volunteer in January of 1975.

"I just did it for the opportunity to do some extra skating," Pare says. "Then I was invited into the OHA, and then earned a job in the IHL when it was headquartered in Windsor, in the fall of '76. I did that for three years; earned a lot of exposure from that and the OHA."

Of course, exposure only benefits those that have nailed down the basics. To be given the opportunity to develop into a Scampy, one must possess characteristics and abilities to leapfrog the competition early on. Aside from good skating skills, good hand-eye coordination, and the ability to make snap decisions, officials must possess a number of intangibles to set themselves apart.

"I think being honest with players is the key," says Pare. "You're better off owning up to a mistake if you make one, as opposed to trying to lie your way out of it. You also have to be honest with your fellow officials."

Pare recalls a perfect example from his NHL career.

"Terry Ruskowski of Chicago was in the offensive zone on the penalty kill," Pare explains. "He was coming back out as his teammate was pushing the puck back in. He hadn't made it out yet when the puck was headed toward him and I blew the whistle. The problem was, at that moment he reached out over the line and stopped the puck before it touched the blue line and crossed. The puck never crossed in, and he would have been able to kill off more of the penalty. I blew it."

Pare looked at Ruskowski and said, "Boy, you fooled me there. I completely screwed that up."

"Don't worry about it," Rosko answered.

"That's one of those moments when you want to find a place to hide. Everybody is watching. They know it wasn't offside, but I'm blowing the whistle. I jumped the gun, but I was honest and moved on," Pare concludes.

"Lie and you lose respect," points out referee Bill McCreary. "I remember working a game with Scampy in LA when I made a too-many-men-on-the-ice call. Unfortunately for me, LA's opponent had actually pulled their goalie. I explained my screw-up to Kings coach Larry Robinson, and didn't have to endure too much criticism because he's such a class guy. I admitted I screwed up and actually *didn't* give LA the power play. We moved on."

"They definitely had six guys out there, but the goalie was sittin' on the bench," Scampy laughs. It was one of the very rare situations and occasions where a referee could, and did, actually reverse his call. It wasn't a subjective call at all; it was black and white, and the play was treated as a quick whistle. A face-off occurred where play had stopped.

Of course, not everyone, nor every situation, is so forgiving. Insults fly from all directions. Bryan Lewis remembers a comment he received from Al Coates, then GM in Calgary.

"I'll pay to fly [linesman] Randy Mitton anywhere you want, just as long as Mitton's not working in Calgary," Coates uttered to Lewis. A comment like that carries connotations of consistent incompetence, even though it may have just come from frustration built over one night, or from something personal.

"Thick skin is really important," adds NHL linesman Brad Kovachik. "I don't get uncomfortable with being yelled at; it comes with the job. You definitely have players that can be unfair to you, but you have to remember, it's part of the game and they're at such a high level, they're so competitive, the juices are flowing. You just have to know when to draw the line. I truly think officiating is something where you have it or you don't," Kovachik considers. "If you let things bother you, if you let things fester for a week because you blew a call, that's not good criteria for an official. You have to have a very short memory."

Scampy always tells young officials, "You're going to miss a call here and there; you have to let it go."

"Even if you screw something up, and you take some heat," Pare says, "you can still earn respect. By showing you care, by always being alert and energetic, and by showing up every night, even if you're not the most talented, you'll earn respect. Just like players, some of the most talented officials don't give it their all every night, and maybe they don't make it."

Once they do make it to the NHL, officials have to deal with a rulebook that is constantly morphing. The greatest example of interpretation trauma came back in the early seventies, with referee Wally Harris and linesmen John D'Amico and Scampy in St. Louis.

"It was the start of the playoffs. The League had just come out of its meetings, and they thought they had the ultimate solution to penalty minutes," remembers Harris. "As it stood, if you got a five-on-four, with a five-minute penalty on one side and a double-minor on the other, the team with the eventual power play would have to wait four minutes for the one-minute advantage to start. Problem was, if you were in the last five minutes of the game, the one team would never get the power play."

Harris interpreted the League directive as wanting to preserve the integrity of the power play.

"If that's what you want, fine!" Wally told his bosses.

In the first playoff game, Harris handed out a five-minute major for high-sticking and five for fighting to one guy, and two minutes for high-sticking and five for fighting for the opponent. Harris decided to put three minutes on the board, a power play that would start ticking immediately. Confusion ensued.

"Scampy and D'Amico wouldn't drop the puck," Harris recalls.

CHAPTER 5

"You can't put three minutes on the board, Wally,"
D'Amico urged.

"Just drop the bloody puck," Harris said after a lengthy
discussion.

It was the first time three minutes had ever gone up
on the penalty board. After a discussion between Harris,
St. Louis coach Scotty Bowman, and New York coach
Emile Francis, the three agreed.

"That's what the League said," they decided.

After the game, phone calls came in from everyone.

"How can a senior referee put three minutes on the
board?" questioned Scotty Morrison.

"Can you tell me the difference between ten and
seven?" Harris answered with a question. Both linesmen
were worried for the next game, while Harris admitted
feeling uncomfortable with the interpretation.

"I'm in shit up to my eyebrows," he said. "I'm going to
pay for this." Which indeed he did—the League fined him.

"If this happens again tonight, I'm going back to the old
rules," he said. During that time, everyone referred to his
penalty clock interpretation as the "Wally Rule." Ironically,
in 2003, the NHL adopted a penalty policy that essentially
upholds the Wally Rule. The power play time is awarded
immediately, and the differential is put on the clock.

"It's idiotic," Harris concludes. "They change the rules
every other year." Harris should know. After ref'ing, he
worked as the Assistant Director of Officials for ten years,
and then as a supervisor.

Besides working for several supervisors, directors, and vice presidents, Scampy has worked for four different ultimate bosses during all of these changes: NHL Presidents Clarence Campbell, John Ziegler, and Gil Stein briefly, and then-Commissioner Gary Bettman. And, as the old cliché goes, the more things change, the more they stay the same.

"A few years ago, Scotty Morrison had a retirement dinner at the great hall in the Hockey Hall of Fame," Scampy recalls. "I'm eating. Ziegler's there, he's eating. Ziegler's smiling. He's waving. Finally, a few minutes later, maybe on the way to the men's room, Ziegler leans over to me and says, "Ron, you're still at it, eh?"

"Yeah, still at it ... ," Scampy answered, "[under his breath] you weenie."

"Usually I was mistaken for John [D'Amico], not Ron. Ron nobody, he just didn't get my name right," Scampy concludes.

Thankless anonymity.

A Brotherhood of Pranksters

I don't think there's a pair of pliers big enough in this world to pull that smile off his face. Scampy just loves being around the game.
—Frank Brown, NHL Vice President of Media Relations

A wonderful way to break up the monotony of travel and relieve the pressure of game nights is to screw around. Hockey is a boys' game played by men, and nowhere else does the term "boys will be boys" fit better. If the Hockey Hall of Fame had a practical joker category, Scampy would be the first official inducted. On or off the ice, he rarely missed an opportunity to deliver a witty remark or play a prank on someone.

Example one of the many that follow involves former Islanders coach Al Arbour. The Cup-winning bench boss hated referee Ron Wicks. "Radar" thought "Wicksy" was the worst ref ever to lace up a pair of skates. They both hailed from the same town outside of Sudbury, Ontario.

"Regardless of how much grief coaches and managers tried to give Wicks on occasion," Scampy explains, "Hall of Fame official and NHL bigwig Frank Udvari would be there to smooth things over with the various hockey people. Udvari had gained incredible respect and he had a soft spot in his heart for Wicksy."

One night, Arbour was coaching the Islanders against the Sabres at Buffalo. Scampy worked the game with referee Richard Trottier.

"I'm on the blue line right in front of Al," Scampy tells it, "and Trottier's in the corner."

Arbour's yelling at him. "Trottier, you're brutal, you're the worst ref I've ever seen, you're f——ing terrible. You're the worst I've ever seen."

Scampy had his hands on his hips. He looked around at Arbour and said, "Al, what about Wicksy?"

Arbour laughed and began yelling towards the corner again. "Trottier, you're the second-worst referee I've ever seen."

~

Long before he oversaw NHL officialdom, Bryan Lewis began as an NHL ref in 1970. His first game was at the Montreal Forum.

"Obviously the staff was much smaller back then … we had a great deal of camaraderie … everyone knew each other's families and such," Lewis says. "The screwing around was pretty consistent as well, and Scampy was really good at it, although, better at giving than receiving.

"Let's say the new guy went to supper. We'd try to get into his room, remove all of the furniture—even light bulbs—and stack it in the stairwell. Scampy knew it was coming; he'd tell the front desk not to give anyone his key. We finally got him in Philly. Told him we were going to the movies, waited for him to leave, and moved all of his stuff. He wouldn't admit it happened.

CHAPTER 6

"Another welcome for new guys was to put shaving cream in their boots at the rink," Lewis says. "My favorite was a trick we pulled on Will Norris a couple times. On long flights, Toronto to LA or something, Scampy and I would rip all of the "free-trial subscription" coupons out of the magazines, fill in Willie's name and address, and then drop them in a mailbox once we landed.

"Scampy was a little bugger," Lewis adds, "but I don't remember him doing anything harmful, or hurtful, or anything to hurt anyone's job. The worst he ever did to me? He put some goop on my windshield, so when I turned on the wipers, I couldn't see a damn thing. I got him back by disconnecting four of his spark plug wires."

~

When long-time NHL security chief Al Wiseman passed away a few years ago, most of the stories at Wiseman's funeral involved Scampy. The two had a career-long game of Tom and Jerry, without the trauma and dismemberment. Al, at six foot three and at least 230 pounds, and Scampy, about five foot seven and a buck-seventy soaking wet, went at it constantly, with Al usually being the victim of "that little shit's" latest ruse. And it's not that Al didn't love it, because he did. It was part of the camaraderie that makes life in hockey so wonderful.

Wiseman wasn't Jewish, but apparently his name sounded Jewish, so Scampy would find out what flight Al was on during the playoffs, call the airline, and order him a kosher meal. To get even, Al would sneak into the officials' dressing room in Toronto, tape a picture of Scampy to a step ladder, and place it in front of the urinal. This just scratched the surface.

~

The aiders and abettors to the shenanigans of these two gentlemen were sometimes a surprise, like Scotty Morrison, for example. Eventually the long-time president of the Hockey Hall of Fame, Morrison used to be the vice president in charge of the officials at the NHL. He always kept his distance from any off-ice tomfoolery, while keeping his respectful distinction as "the boss" intact.

"Back when Edmonton played at their finest, the security chief there, a former long-time RCMP for twenty-five years, used to throw a party or barbecue at his house during an off day of the Finals," Morrison begins. "He'd invite officials, a bunch of ex-RCMPs, and he'd invite me. Usually, I'd politely decline."

One year, Morrison decided what the heck, he'd make the event.

"The Stanley Cup was there, sitting on red felt, on a table," Morrison points out. "Al Wiseman, responsible for the Stanley Cup, and Frank Torpey, the security man out of New York, were both on hand. Two or three of the young Mounties came to me and said, 'We're going to have some fun. When they're not looking, the Stanley Cup is going to disappear.'" Naturally, Scampy was in on this little scheme.

"Al, before you and Frank take the Cup back to the hotel," Scampy started, "can we get a couple pictures with it?" Wiseman happily obliged, but when he turned around, Lord Stanley's holy grail had vanished.

"Hey, smart guy!" Wiseman raised his voice.

"What?" Scampy reacted.

"Where's the Cup?" Wiseman asked.

Scampy turned, "Oh my God, what happened? Where's the Cup?"

Everyone shrugged. Morrison, in on the joke, did his best imitation of NHL President John Ziegler on-ice.

"I'd really love to present you with the Stanley Cup," Morrison said mimicking Ziegler, "but, we don't know where the hell it is."

Wiseman smiled but grew impatient. The officials declared that because of the upcoming game the next day, they had to get back to the hotel.

"Hey, no one's leaving until I get that Cup!" Wiseman said.

"No one seems to know where it is," Scampy said.

"You little son of a bitch," Al said smiling, and he picked up Scampy and held him as high as he could. "How are you getting back?" he asked Scampy.

"We rented a car, we rented a car," Scampy answered. Wiseman carried Ray to the car, set him down, ordered him to open the trunk, and there it was.

The officials had planned on taking it back to the hotel to keep it until the next day and make the security boys really squirm. Wiseman's detective experience solved the spoof almost immediately.

"Once he knew Scampy was driving, he knew where the Cup was," Morrison concludes.

∽

One time, on a flight, both Scampy and Wiseman were in business class. Al was in row two; Scampy was a couple rows back. Al stood up to make his way to the restroom, turned to Scampy, and showed him the mini salt and pepper shakers that came with the meal.

"Oh Ray, I love these things. My wife and I use them for our Bloody Marys in the summertime," Al said.

Al put them in his lapel pocket. When Al stepped into the head, Scampy summoned the flight attendant.

"Do you have a sense of humor?"

"Yes," she answered, smiling.

"Well, you know that big, tall, dopey bastard in the second row? He stole the salt and pepper shakers and put them in his breast pocket, so when you pick up the tray, ask him about the shakers."

Al Strachan and a few other media types up front were in on it, just waiting for Wiseman to get popped.

After relieving himself, Wiseman nudged his way back to his seat. Moments later, the flight attendant stopped to pick up Al's tray with a concerned look on her face.

"Where are the salt and pepper shakers, sir?" Al paused, turned red, reached into his pocket, pulled out the shakers, and handed them to her.

The flight attendant burst out laughing.

Al turned around to Scampy and howled, "You little bastard!"

"Scampy and Al were both avid golfers," remembers retired linesman Ron Foyt. "They'd send each other gag gifts at Christmas. Ray sent him broken clubs ... sent him Titleist golf balls that were cracked and hacked and rewrapped. They used to wrap up old shirts and pants as gifts."

～

Standard minor league tricks were common. When Al fell asleep on the plane, Scampy would tie Wiseman's shoelaces to the bottom of the seat in front of him.

When Wiseman quit smoking, Scampy went out of his way to make it a bit tough on him. At one point, the two bet on whether Al could actually quit. In Chicago, after making the wager, Scampy bought two packs of cigarettes and taped the individual darts all over the interior of Wiseman's rental car. Honest to a fault, Wiseman paid up every time he slipped.

"I remember Al always used to wear this same pair of gray slacks, and it always seemed when Al came out of the bathroom, he'd always have little wet spots on the crotch. I'm not sure if it was water from the faucet, or if he just hadn't finished the job," Scampy laughs. "So I bought him one of those little handheld fans, to help dry off his dribble every time he came out of the bathroom."

No wonder the guy died; he was continuously harassed by a maniacal imp.

"I miss Al a lot. He was the kind of guy you loved to have around," Scampy concludes.

～

Joe Caporiccio was another security guy who often took grief. Second in command in New York, he'd travel around to the Stanley Cup Finals. Bob Hartley, when he coached

Colorado, had set up a round of golf at his private club for a few of the NHL boys. Scampy, Caporiccio, and six others were on the list to enjoy the match.

"We didn't know how well everyone played," Scampy explains, "so we didn't know how many strokes to give Joe."

"I'll go to the range and see how he hits 'em," Scampy volunteered at the time. Caporiccio was on the practice tee, wearing a button-down white dress shirt, and he wasn't hitting them very well at all.

Scampy yelled across, "Hey Joe, instead of playing, why don't you just go grab us some sandwiches."

"F——k you, Scampy," came the reply.

Was he sandbagging?

"No, he was a bad golfer," Scampy laughs. "We had a wonderful time, though."

~

Linesman Wayne Bonney remembers Scampy always pulling his leg, at one point, literally.

"In 1990, I had hurt my leg," Bonney recalls. (Years later, he'd have hip replacement surgery.) "At the time, as always, Scamp was doing little practical jokes. On the ice, one of his favorites was to fool the other officials into thinking there was a fight. We'd be kind of standing there after a whistle and Scampy would suddenly get a serious look on his face and burst off in an odd direction, trying to make it look like he was going to break something up. So I'd react by lunging or leaping in that direction, only to find out nothing had happened. Once in New York he did it, and I had a little twitch in my leg, and I said 'Raymond, please don't do that, my leg hurts and I don't want to wreck it anymore.'"

Next period, Scampy did it again.

"I took the puck and whipped it at his nuts," Bonney laughs.

"Okay, okay," Scampy said. "I won't do it again."

"Scampy was famous for doing the fake," recalls linesman Scott Driscoll. "He got me once or twice with that. He'd come get the puck and skate away real quick, like something was going on. It was like *Peter and the Wolf*."

"You know, that was a cruel joke for linesmen, but it was practical for referees," points out ref Stephen Walkom. "I noticed a few times he did it to make sure our focus was where it should be. He'd get your attention towards the players' benches if you weren't looking there already.

"Another one of his famous tricks," continues Walkom, "was to mess with you during a major issue or a confrontation with a player or coach. Let's say Tie Domi came over and was complaining about a call, you're going through your explanation—back when we were allowed to talk—and Scampy would skate over all serious, like he was going to move the player. Then he'd surprise us."

"That was a terrible tripping call, wasn't it Tie?" Scampy would offer.

"Yeah. See? Even Scampy thought it sucked," Domi would chime in.

"This doesn't sound like the most supportive thing to do," Walkom continues, "but it was so off the wall, it would break the tension. He was great at picking the right time for that. Along those lines, he was very good at keeping the room relaxed before a game. He had a calm confidence, and always seemed to pick the right time to be serious or to joke."

Referee Paul Devorski concurs.

"He's awful with his jokes," Devo adds. "He's relaxed and he keeps me relaxed because he's always yelling goofy shit. All of a sudden you're in a real serious mode, I'll have my arm up to call a penalty, then I'll call the penalty on the guy, and he'll come skating in and stop. He'll look at me and say, 'You're not calling that horseshit penalty, are you?' The whole team is looking at you, he skates away laughing, and they don't know whether to take him seriously or not."

Linesman Scott Driscoll recalls similar behavior.

"I remember in Toronto once," Driscoll says, "I had a decision to make: whether to make an intentional offside or a regular offside call. I decided to call it a regular offside."

Immediately, players started to pipe in, "That's gotta be all the way down, c'mon."

"Just as the players are in the middle of bitching," Driscoll continues, "Scampy comes flying in and says 'why isn't that all the way down?' He was just a little shit, throwing a match on the fire."

"Hey, listen to Scamp," the players would urge.

"That wasn't offside," Driscoll mimics Scampy. "Who's offside there?"

"He was always screwing around, and because of his speed, and more so his anticipation, I'd always try to challenge him to races," Driscoll says. "We'd race to a puck at one end, he'd win, and say, 'What happen? You fall down?'"

It didn't take linesman Brad Kovachik long to learn Scampy's tricks.

"One of my first games, in Buffalo against Pittsburgh, the first night I met Raymond, I didn't know what to think about him or anything," Kovey says. "I made an early close call at my blue line, an offside call. Being a young guy, all of the players were in my face yelling at me, screaming that I shouldn't have called it."

"What were you looking at?" they yelled.

"Three players were beside me, Ray comes skating up, stops, glances at the players real quick, looks at me, and says, 'Brad, what'd you blow your whistle for?' The players started laughing and it broke up a little bit of a tense situation. I'll never forget that game," Kovey concludes. "Pat Lafontaine got whacked pretty good in open ice and was out for a year or two."

During Scampy's final season, Walkom finally got him back for all of his wisecracks and trickery.

"After he shaved his head," Walkom remembers, "I told him, 'It's about time. After all these years you lost the comb-over, and cut it down to the wood.'"

"I didn't have a comb-over," Scampy would answer.

"In early 2004, I discovered an old Scampy hockey card, and sure enough, comb-over," Walkom concludes.

~

Another example of returning the favor came from NHL VP Jim Gregory. During training camp prior to the

1993–94 season, the Rangers and Maple Leafs played exhibition games in London, England. Gregory, then a supervisor, the officials—Scampy, Leon Stickle and Denis Morel—and the teams stayed for almost a week at a four-star hotel with a fancy restaurant.

"The games were over at about 10, 10:30, so we probably didn't get out of the rink until about 11," Scampy recalls. "All week, we had a bit of a tough time finding a good meal that time of night, so on the final night, Gregory made arrangements to keep the dining room open at the hotel. Of course, fancy schmancy food in a fancy schmancy hotel can get particularly expensive."

"There were probably a dozen or so people eating," Gregory recalls. "Morel's wife, Debbie, was there, a few other friends and family. So when the bill came, I said 'Ray, you pick it up.'"

"I didn't say anything," Scampy recalls. "I'd been in London, all expenses paid for the most part by the League, staying at a nice place, not much to complain about."

Getting over his initial shock, Scampy grabbed hold of the bill. Converting from British sterling to Canadian dollars, the bill came to about eleven hundred bucks without gratuity. Scampy pulled out his Visa and paid the tab.

"We were flying out the next morning. I went back to my room and was thinking, 'Man oh man, thirteen hundred bucks!'"

An hour later, the phone rang. Scampy answered it, "Oh God, I hope this is Jim Gregory." Gregory burst out laughing on the other end.

Chapter 6

"Put the dinner on your expenses," the boss said.

"Oh my, thanks Jim," replied Scampy.

"From there, the officials went to our training camp, and Gregory must have shared that story a half-dozen times," Scampy concludes.

Scampy is legendary for being frugal. Rob Shick remembers one occasion in Edmonton.

"We were walking down the street, on an afternoon colder than a well-digger's ass, when a street guy comes up to Scampy," Shick relates.

"Excuse me sir, do you have fifty cents so I can catch the bus?" the man asked as he held out a Styrofoam coffee cup.

"If you hadn't spent the money on the coffee," Scampy retorted, "You'd have money for the bus."

"He's probably the only guy that had one of those New York taxi cab flags installed in his car," jokes Leon Stickle of Scampy. "He'd flip it up when he'd drive to games, to make sure he wasn't going to miss recording kilometers."

"Early in my career, a tradition after lunch was to go out and get ice cream," recalls ref Bill McCreary. "Scampy would let us flip the coin to see who'd buy the ice cream. This was back during the three-man system. We'd all go, and he'd always win the round robin. Unbeknown to us, Scampy had bought a two-headed coin. He'd always recommend we go for an ice cream, and he'd always win. It was the ice cream coin."

"When Scampy would pay his fair share, he'd often whine about it," laughs his friend and fellow linesman Mark Pare.

"About six or seven years ago, I remember we got to play Doral in Florida," Pare continues. "We knew some of the teaching pros down there at Jim McLean's golf school. We'd always get the greens fees comp'd. Naturally, we wanted to play the Blue Monster, where they play the tournament there, but this one time they had us booked on one of the other Doral courses."

Pare went by the starter's shed and asked if there was any way the two of them could play the Blue Monster. Pare had forty bucks in his hand, which he gave to the starter, who responded with, "You're up."

"I got us on the Blue Monster," Pare told Scampy, "but it cost me forty bucks, so it's going to cost you twenty." Scampy went into mock shock, and ragged on Pare the whole round and wouldn't let up.

"The green fees were probably $250, and we were playing for twenty, but Scampy wouldn't let it go," Pare says.

"Who else you gonna tip?" Scampy probed.

The two of them walked by a guy working in the pro shop.

"Hey, you wanna tip that guy? Did you tip that guy yet?" Scampy questioned Pare.

The two of them arrived back at the hotel, and the doorman held the door open for them.

"Hey Pare, you'd better tip this guy," Scampy urged.

"He was relentless," Pare says. "He couldn't stop busting."

"Mark's incredibly organized and active," Scampy says. "He's renowned for doing the laundry, arranging things, and booking tee times. We get along very well. I'd work every one of my games with Mark Pare, and it's not just off the ice. If I had to pick a guy to work a seventh game with, I'd pick Mark. He's a real solid linesman, technically sound."

"You'd never know what you'd get from him on the golf course," Pare starts again. "Out in California, when we were on the ice in Anaheim, we asked [player] Warren Reichel, who I knew from outside Windsor, where we should go for golf connections."

"I can hook you up at Pelican Hills at Newport Beach," Reichel answered. "The comptroller there is from Windsor. As it turned out, Pare knew the man as well, and had actually lined some of his brother's junior games.

"We're standing on this wind-blown tee, a par-three along the ocean," Pare remembers. "Ray and I are staring at this huge house being built over the water near the tee. The course is pretty quiet, there's very few people around, so Ray jumped over a little fence and began walking up to the electrician.

"C'mon," Ray ordered Pare.

"Alright," Pare followed.

"Who's the contractor?" Ray asked the electrician with authority.

"Mike," the man answered.

"Mike!" Ray yelled, as he started walking through the house. "Mi-ike!" Pare followed him, until he found the builder.

"Ray starts telling this guy that he and his wife were looking to buy and build in the area," Pare recalls. "I started giggling. Ray shot me a dirty look, and before you know it, he's getting the grand tour of this unbelievable house. I went back to the cart."

"The walk-in closets were bigger than most of the rooms in my house," Ray said at the time. It was a fifteen thousand square foot house, the lot cost $2.2 million at the time, and the house cost another $4 million plus. Ray simply wanted to have a look.

~

Stephen Walkom used to call Scampy the Squirrel.

"One of these days he'll go around and dig up all those tins of money he has buried," jokes Walks.

Scott Driscoll has had three nicknames. One is Cub, because in the early part of his career, his mentor was Ron Asselstine, known as Bear. They were roommates during Driscoll's first training camp.

"Here comes Bear and his little Cub," ref Rob Shick would say.

Driscoll was also known as Hop Sing because he always volunteered to do laundry on the road. Scampy also called him Cosmo, after the character Cosmo Kramer on *Seinfeld*. The two linesmen shared a love for the show and would swap tapes of their favorite episodes.

Retired linesman Wayne Bonney's nickname is Buckwheat. In 1972, working in the minors in Charlotte, North Carolina, Bonney was ready to drop the puck during the second period but there was a delay. The referee was conferring with the off-ice officials at the penalty box. The Independence Arena was packed with patrons, and since this was years before blaring music became the norm during stoppages, one could hear the chatter and the ebb and flow of the crowd's banter and noise. Growing impatient over the delay, one country bumpkin stood up and yelled, "Drop the Goddamn puck, Buckwheat." The ref blew his whistle, came over, and said, "That's your name from now on ... Buckwheat."

To this day even Bonney's daughter calls him by the nickname.

Paul Devorski's nickname wasn't always Devo, the simple short version of his name. Years earlier, as a junior player, he remembers being called Dork, a reflection of his on-ice tendencies. Then it became Dukie because he fought a lot, but when he came to the NHL, linesman Leon Stickle already had that moniker, so Devorski was switched to Devo. Stickle's other nickname is Stick, while Dukie remains unexplained.

Scampy's nickname for linesman Mark Pare is Chummo.

"Ray could never remember names in rinks." Pare recalls. "We'd walk into a building and everyone would recognize him. They'd say, 'Hi Ray' to him, and just nod at me. Ray would say, 'Hey buddy, hey pal, what's up?'

"The joke became he'd be Palsy, I'd be Chummo. We just gave ourselves those names," Pare continues. "I'd remember everybody's name but they wouldn't know mine; he wouldn't remember theirs but they'd remember his."

"I'm brutal with people's names," Ray says.

A bonus nickname for Ray came from Toronto Maple Leaf broadcasters Joe Bowen and Harry Neale.

"Just to watch him," starts Bowen, "the thing we've always loved is his enthusiasm, his mad dash from one end to the other on his icings, and his professionalism. Veal Scaloppini—Harry [Neale] started that, kind of nicknamed him that based on his Italian background. Now when we see him, we just call him Veal."

"Scampy often brought people to the game," Neale recalls. "He'd bring them to the booth beforehand, and we liked that. We often iso'ed [isolated him on camera] Scampy. He was often wanting us to mention his son's hockey team or some guy that he knew that had something to do with Guelph ... sick, married, or something. Especially during a slow game, we'd talk about Scampy, show him on an icing. Look at Veal go!"

Rob Shick, "Shicker," sums up the nickname business: "In Philadelphia, I had a lot of other nicknames ... you can start with every letter of the alphabet."

~

Bonney really let rookie linesman Baron Parker have it once.

Rookies did laundry.

"Let me have your stuff. I'll wash it," Parker told Bonney when they had returned to the hotel after a game in San Jose. They were doing back-to-back games there.

An hour or so after he parted with his jersey, Bonney went to the laundry room himself to get it back. With no one around, Bonney looked in the dryer, saw his jersey, grabbed it, figured it was dry enough, and walked upstairs.

"I hid it. He didn't know I had it, so I hid it. I actually gave it to the referee."

Not much later Parker showed up at Bonney's room.

"Here's your stuff, ahhh, but there's a problem," Parker started.

"What's the problem?" Bonney asked, knowing full well.

"I don't have the jersey," Parker replied.

"What do you mean you don't have the jersey? I gave it to you," Bonney pressed.

"Yeah, I know, but I can't find it," Parker said.

"Do you have yours?"

"Yeah, I've got everything, I just can't find your jersey," Parker admitted again.

"We've got a game tomorrow night at seven o'clock. You've got one day to find me a jersey. If you don't find me a jersey by game time, I'm wearing your jersey and you're going to wear a white practice jersey from the team." Bonney was exercising seniority.

"No way," Parker came back.

"Oh yeah," Bonney insisted.

Bonney got a good night's sleep, woke up, and kind of forgot about the hazing-in-progress until Parker showed up at his room.

Parker started searching the room for Bonney's jersey.

"What are you doing?" Bonney asked innocently.

"I'm checking your room," Parker responded, thinking he was on to something. He was, of course, but Bonney wasn't yet ready to let him off the hook. Parker had a nervous smile. Bonney played dumb.

Along came pre-game at the rink.

"Where's my jersey?" Bonney asked Parker.

"I don't have it," Parker answered.

"That's it, give me your jersey." Bonney pulled rank and Parker obliged. Bonney then instructed the security guard, who already knew about the prank, to go get Parker a white jersey.

At that point, Parker tried to explain the lost jersey to his cohorts. He ran through the scenario again and again, and concluded someone must have ripped it off. The security guard came back, Parker took the white jersey, turned it inside out, and pulled it on. The referee led the linesmen down a tunnel and toward the ice to get loose, check the nets, and get the game started. Parker pulled up the rear, wearing his white jersey.

Just before they stepped onto the ice, Bonney stopped.

"I forgot my whistle, damn it. How did I forget my whistle?" Bonney shouted. He turned around and headed back toward the dressing room. Parker stepped past him and hit the ice, and started skating around in the inside-out practice jersey. Bonney went back to the room, pulled out his own linesman sweater and put it on. He took Parker's jersey and handed it to the security guard as he stepped back onto the ice.

As the officials and players stood in the dark for the introductions and the national anthem, Parker felt like an idiot in his white jersey. Meanwhile, Bonney had a fat smirk on his face. As the lights came on, Parker was getting in position for the start of the game when Bonney pointed to the glass at the Zamboni gate. On cue, the security guard waved around Parker's jersey.

"Look what I found," the guard mouthed.

More relieved at that point than angry, Parker cursed out Bonney under his breath, headed to the corner, and swapped shirts.

"The only reason I gave you that jersey back," Bonney explained, "is because [NHL Commissioner] Bettman is watching the game."

~

Mark Pare shares his three favorite Scampy stories:

"First, he was a fun guy to work with, always upbeat, always up for a game of golf, going for a walk, or just people-watching," Pare begins. "He always was a good guy to travel with because he just couldn't sit still.

"In Pittsburgh once, a group of us were going out for lunch. We walked into a restaurant and there was a table full of ladies, probably about eight of them. It was obviously an office lunch or something. They were talking about a thousand miles an hour. Ray walked over and sat down and started taking off his jacket."

"Sorry I'm late," Ray said. "There was a lot of bad traffic—there was an accident. What did I miss?"

The girls all looked at him like, where the hell did this guy come from?

"So what are we ordering?" Ray pressed on.

They looked at him.

"Oh sorry, wrong table," Ray said as he got up.

"He got up and walked away," Pare says. "The other linesmen were laughing hard; the women had their mouths open. He was always good with that stuff."

Pare tells his second favorite Ray tale.

"Sitting with a group of two or three on the airplane, he'd have a newspaper in front of his face, reading it to a young guy," Pare recalls.

"Last night's game was a rough one," Ray would pretend to read. "It was probably headed in the direction of a 'pier-six brawl' if it wasn't for the cool-headed efforts of linesman Mark Pare. Pare took the bull by the horns and made sure none of the nonsense escalated."

"Ray would keep on reading, while the young linesman would sit there with his mouth agape.

"No way," the kid would say.

Ray would add the finish, "Pat Quinn commented after the game, 'This is a shining example of what an official should be.'"

"Holy shit," came the reaction.

The last of Pare's favorite three stories are of events that took place in Maple Leaf Gardens.

"Kirk Muller is playing for Toronto at the time. Mats Sundin just scored a goal," Pare starts. "For whatever reason, the referee is over at the penalty box. I'm not sure if the goal was being reviewed or not. Scampy and I are standing in front of the Leafs' bench as the team is high-fiving and celebrating. The ref's still not at center ice and Scampy gets this serious look on his face."

"What's up, Scamp?" Muller asks.

"First of all, the goal that was scored was disallowed, and Kirk, you've got a major for spearing," Scampy said matter-of-factly.

"Muller eyes became saucers," Pare remembers. "Deadpan, Ray keeps looking at him, as if the ref was about to skate up at any moment from behind and order Muller into the box. Sundin was the first to realize Scampy was kidding."

"I'm gonna punch you," Sundin said to Scampy.

"Muller saw Sundin smile and Scampy smile, laugh, and skate aside, and did a couple double takes back and forth between Scampy and the bench."

"Shit!" Muller said with a relieved smile.

Bill McCreary remembers a solid jab back from Sundin.

"Me and Scamp did the last game at Maple Leaf Gardens when Chicago was in town," McCreary remembers. "Mush Marsh was a hockey legend. He had scored the first goal ever at the Gardens. So the last night, they ushered him out to drop the first puck. Sundin skates up and says to Scampy, 'So Scampy, how was Mush as a face-off guy?'"

Other players took greater liberties with their jokes. The home team equipment guys are the ones who sharpen skates for the officials. Scampy wears a size five-and-a-half. Canadiens defenseman Serge Savard once came across Scampy's skates in Montreal and wrote on them with a magic marker, "Where'd you get these, Toys "R" Us?"

Doug Gilmour took it one step further. He melted the plastic lace holes on Scampy's skates. Scampy couldn't get laces through them. Not that he needed to; one of the phenomenal things about Scampy's skating speed and ability is the fact that he can whirl around effectively without skate laces. In NHL games he wore them, but only tight enough so that they stayed tied and they didn't drag on the ice.

"I don't know what to say," Scampy declares. "I guess I have weird feet. My feet and skates have kind of become one and the same."

"I'd see those loose laces when I was the backup on the bench," remembers former goalie turned TV commentator Glen Healey, "and I'd say to Ray, 'What's a matter, battlin' the gout?' I'd say it every time. He'd give me a look."

"Players were comfortable with him, officials were comfortable with him, and so were coaches," McCreary says. "You'd love to have Scampy as a brother. He'd always screw around. In the airport, he'd do the dollar-bill-on-the-string thing. He'd pull it away from travelers as they went to reach for it. That attitude translated on the ice when needed. He'd do a lot of little things to help a referee—make a joke at the right time, calm a situation."

McCreary's 1,000th game was at Air Canada Centre. His family was there for it, and the milestone was announced in the rink.

Scampy skates over to Leafs coach Pat Quinn. "Hey," Scampy shouts, "I didn't see you clapping for Billy."

"Quinn goes, 'Hey!' and gives me a thumbs up," McCreary remembers. "That's the kind of respect and admiration those guys have for Scampy."

"The NHL was always giving out ivory carvings to players," remembers former linesman Ron Foyt, "or Eskimo carvings, whatever, for anniversaries, consecutive games played, that kind of thing. The officials usually didn't get squat for milestones. When Randy Mitton did his 1,500th game in Edmonton, Ray carved a puck out of a bar of ivory soap. The local TV guys came down there, Scampy presented it to him, and it was priceless. Ray never took himself too serious," Foyt concludes. "He took his job serious, but not himself."

"There's a fine line, actually a pretty broad line, you can't cross when it comes to joking around," Scampy points out. "Like when a guy screws up a call, for example. There's no way you're going to bust his balls about it; you're going to help him out. You're not going to give a guy crap, throw him under the bus in front of his peers, especially since the next screwy call might be yours. No joking there."

"Constructive criticism, even if kind of funny, is okay," mentions Ron Foyt. "One time with Ray, I was having a hard time with face-offs for whatever reason. Obviously, they're critical, like a pitcher throwing a ball. You don't want to have a bad face-off. The one night, I had no rhythm, players started to get mad … even the fans were booing."

"You're making the players mad, the fans mad, and now you're making me mad," Scampy offered up.

"I bared down, got it in sync," Foyt concludes.

❧

"Roger Doucet sang at the All-Star Game in Detroit in 1981 when Gordie Howe came back," Scampy remembers. "We had a curtain in the officials' room for some reason, and he stood behind it and sang the anthem, while I stood in front and mouthed it. That was a cool way of doing karaoke," Scampy smiles.

Before that same game, Barry Bremen, at the time known as "the great imposter" who had dressed for an NBA game and made it on the court for a shoot-around, and dressed in drag and hopped onto an NFL field as a Dallas Cowboys cheerleader, tried to sneak on the ice dressed as an official.

"He came up behind us in the tunnel," Scampy recalls. "John D'Amico spotted him."

"Where do you think you're going?" linesman D'Amico said.

"I'm going to check the nets," Bremen answered.

"You're not going anywhere," D'Amico said.

"He called security and the guy never got on the ice," Scampy concludes.

~

Traveling with Scampy could be an adventure, according to Paul Devorski.

"For games on Long Island, a lot of the officials preferred to spend the day in Manhattan and then train out to Nassau Coliseum and then train back after the game," Devo says. "One night, early in Lance Robert's career, he and Scampy and the ref were riding back on the train to New York."

"Why don't you go back to the café car and get us some drinks and something to eat," Scampy instructed Roberts.

"Sure, Scamp," Roberts replied.

CHAPTER 6

"There goes Lance, up and down the train for about a half an hour," Devo remembers.

"I can't find it," Roberts finally told Scampy after giving up.

There was no cafe car.

Whether riding on steel wheels or rubber, the travel stories abound.

"Another time, I was doing a game in Washington," Scampy says. "Mark Vines, who now owns three or four Tim Hortons, was my partner. The traffic there is ridiculous. We're riding from what's now Reagan Airport to Landover. Vines was driving, and unfortunately, Vinesy drives like he's ninety years old. We stopped the car in the middle of the highway—it was bumper to bumper—did the switch in the middle of the highway, and then I drove like a CIA agent. I was on the shoulder, between cars, holding out my Marriott Hotel card, pretending I was CIA. Cars stopped, swerved; we made it in time.

"I was standby for a playoff game in Calgary," Scampy adds, "John D'Amico tried so hard to get from Edmonton to Calgary during a major snowstorm, he ended up riding a tractor to the rink. Because of all the stress of travel, Scotty Morrison took D'Amico off the game. John was livid, but Scotty wouldn't let him work."

Although Ray always looked up to D'Amico as a linesman, he thought that John as a supervisor was maybe a little too diligent. D'Amico channeled his preparation and thoroughness a little via verbiage.

"He'd come into the officials' room after the game and

speak forever," recalls Ron Foyt. "One night in Boston, Scampy locked the door and kept D'Amico out."

"There's no hollering," Scampy yells through the door, "and you can only stay five minutes and then we're outta here!"

~

Scampy used to imitate the other linesmen. His favorite was "Bear" Ron Asselstine, a big man with plenty of girth and a wide posterior.

"Let's face it, some games are duds," admits Scott Driscoll. "Ray did a great Ron Asselstine. He'd whisper into the air when he was about to drop the puck, push his helmet back, squat down with a wide stance, say something to the guys, drop the puck, and then back out wildly and smash awkwardly into the boards. He'd stretch like Asselstine during the breaks. Ron couldn't skate backwards very well, and he'd waddle. Scampy had it down, and we'd be fricking killing ourselves."

Whether it's related to fellow officials, or players and coaches on the bench, much of the on-ice humor is peripheral. Officials can have a good time just listening in.

"I remember when I came in," starts Mark Pare, "Don Cherry was coaching the expansion team in Colorado. This was after his Boston glory years. He didn't really have to coach the Bruins too much, but he put on a good show. In Colorado, he had to coach a lot, and he'd admonish them a lot. I remember standing in front of the bench one night, and time and time again, he'd be pleading with guys to deliver a check, to shoot."

"Hit somebody, do something out there," Cherry would urge.

"Not funny to him, but the pleading was hilarious," concludes Pare.

"You just never know," states former referee Stephen Walkom. "During the warm-ups at Madison Square Garden, I was skating around in the dark and hit the mat they had laid out at center ice and slid all the way into the corner. It was fresh ice—I couldn't stop. I got up and thought maybe nobody saw ... it was really dark, maybe I got away with it."

Just before the start of the game, Brian Leetch came up to Walkom and said, "You need to work here a few more times so you know where the mat is."

"Good players don't miss anything," Walkom states. "It carries over to the game. If you screw something up, there's a pretty darn good chance everyone noticed."

～

"Since I live nearby, when I was working, I'd get e-mails from guys constantly wanting tickets to Toronto games for friends and family," Scampy remembers. "Dan McCourt ... if you were working a Toronto game, Dan would hit you every time."

Hey guys, I've got a couple people coming down from Copper Cliff. I could use a couple of tickets.

"Screw off," Scampy relives his thoughts. "You don't think I have any friends that need tickets? Give me a break."

The banter goes on and on all year.

"There's a football pool," Scampy points out. "Those guys go back and forth big time."

When Scampy sent out an e-mail to Steve Walkom and about five or six other guys looking for World Cup tickets in September of 2004, he wrote it as follows:

Hi guys, my name is Ray Scapinello. I used to be a linesman in the National Hockey League. I was wondering … if you're not using any of your tickets for the Toronto games, I'd love to purchase two. I can be reached at this e-mail or my number is 519 … "

Responses included *no way, we're using them, not available, f——k off,* and *Ray who?*

"We still joke around," states Rob Shick, "but it won't be the same. It's you and the two or three other guys you're with—that's all you've got most of the time. I've spent a lot of time with Ray over the years. We shared a lot, and I'll miss him."

A typical race to the action during a game between the New Jersey Devils and the Toronto Maple Leafs at the Air Canada Centre in 2004. Scapinello always had incredible speed and almost never did up his skates.

A deft maneuver to clear the way after Ville Nieminen of the Calgary Flames is pushed into the boards by Cory Sarich of the Tampa Bay Lightning during the first overtime in Game Six of the 2004 Stanley Cup Final.

Two thousand five hundred regular season games, 426 playoff contests, and 20 Stanley Cup final series—how many face-offs is that?

Intense concentration, watching the lines.

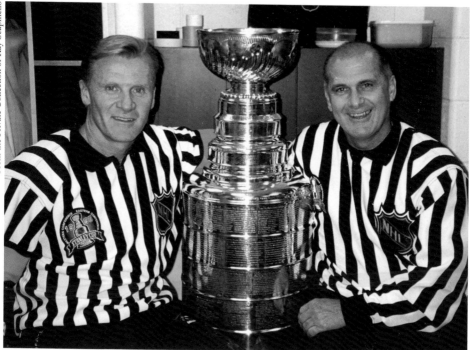

Terry Gregson, the Stanley Cup, and Ray. Gregson and Scampy both worked their final regular-season game of their careers the same night, in Buffalo, in April of 2004.

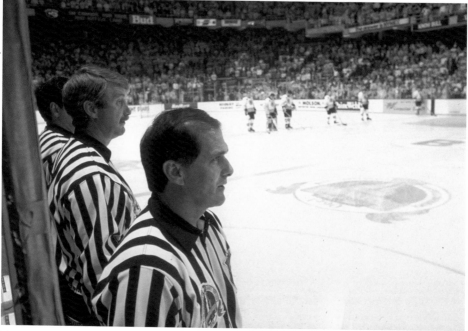

The Zebras. Ray, with his fellow officials, ready for the start of a playoff game. Swede Knox is in the middle.

Left: All in a day's work.

Below: Mending the ice while
Eddie Johnston looks on.

A rare view of Ray wearing a helmet. It was an honor for him to be selected as a linesman for the 1998 Nagano Winter Olympics, where helmets were mandatory equipment.

In his 33-year career, Scampy has had the honor of being on the ice with the greats of the game; here with Wayne Gretzky.

Ray with a full crop of hair. He became more aerodynamic, and more recognizable, after he lost and shaved it.

~ CHAPTER 7 ~

All in the Family

*Scampy was always kind when the opposition scored.
He'd go, "Oh, tough one" or "That wasn't your fault." That
was his way of thanking me because I'd always fish the
puck out of the net for him.*
—Clint Malarchuk, NHL goalie, 1981 to 1992

The universal hockey community is a small one. The "six degrees of separation" theory is reduced to more like one or two degrees within the world of puck—everyone seems to be tied together somewhere. Along those lines, despite the "lack of respect" issue *on* the ice, with players often recklessly getting their sticks up or hitting from behind, the hockey world is a polite and compassionate community, and despite the occasional controversy, officials are as much a part of the clan as anyone else.

To give the perfect example of hockey-as-family, let's start at the top. Wayne Gretzky is known for being many things to many people. He's beyond rock star status in Canada, and over the years he's earned the Great One moniker as much for his off-ice endeavors as for being a wizard on skates.

On Christmas 1995, veteran linesman Wayne Bonney gave his younger brother, Chris, a "Gretzky" LA Kings jersey as a gift. Chris, like any thirty-five-year-old lifelong hockey fan, was thrilled.

"Hey, do you think you could get it autographed?" Chris asked his brother.

"Sure," Wayne answered, "I can give it a shot. I'm headed out west in a couple of weeks."

Meanwhile, Chris would soon be headed into the hospital for a lung transplant. Despite never smoking nor working around asbestos, Chris had developed a rare malady, more difficult to pronounce than to spell, known for being associated with cigarette smoking and asbestos inhalation. His lungs had shrunk down to the size of a boy's fist.

On January 8, Chris's operation was a success, or so it appeared. Hours after his transplant, an air bubble traveled through his bloodstream from his lungs to his brain, causing an aneurysm and killing him instantly. On his 36th birthday, Chris Bonney was dead, leaving behind a family that included two daughters and a ten-year-old son, Kevin.

The family tragedy lingered. Wayne took a week off work, and when it came time to return he indeed, as scheduled, headed out west. He had the Gretzky sweater in hand.

"We were in Calgary, the Kings were visiting, and I was gonna try to get Gretzky to sign the jersey for Kevin," Wayne remembers. "I dropped off the jersey in the LA room, and explained the whole story to the Kings' equipment guy."

During the first intermission, the jersey showed up personalized and signed by Gretzky.

"Thank you, Wayne. That's very kind of you," Bonney told Gretzky on the ice during a break in the second.

In so many words, Gretzky responded, "Kids are special. They make the world go around. You tell him I wish him the best, and let me know if there's anything else you need."

During the second intermission, there was another knock at the officials' door. A Gretzky stick arrived, signed by number 99, and dedicated to Kevin.

"Thank you—you didn't have to do that," Bonney remembers telling Gretzky during the final period.

"You're welcome, and give him my best," Gretzky answered. It was an emotional third period for the linesman, as his mind strayed to his brother.

"Gretzky's unbelievable. The guys can tell you a lot of stories about him like that. He's a great ambassador of the game. I couldn't thank him enough," Bonney says.

Gretzky's as unselfish off the ice as he was on it, all while quietly going about his business.

"Gretzky wasn't a big talker," Scampy says, "but I remember one time doing a game and asking Wayne for a stick. Then wouldn't you know, he gets a misconduct, ten minutes, in the second period, for some reason I don't know," Scampy continues, "and I remember saying to the referee, 'Thank you very much. There goes my hockey stick, you moron.' But after the game, knock on the door, stick boy, autographed stick."

"He's a very classy guy," Scampy says sincerely. "A matter a fact, during the Stanley Cup Finals between LA and Montreal, Wayne set up a round of golf at Sherwood Country Club for Jim Gregory, myself, Bob Cole, and I think Wally Harris. Wayne set it up, with his compliments."

Meeting and dealing with star hockey players is of course cool, but generally taken for granted. Meeting celebrities and famous hockey fans from other sporting endeavors is even cooler.

During those same Stanley Cup Finals, PGA golfer Craig Stadler was at Game Four in LA, sitting with Rangers captain Mark Messier along the glass. Scampy, an absolute golf nut, was the standby linesman for the game, and thought it would be really neat if he could meet the former Masters champ. During the second intermission, Messier had excused himself, so Scampy scooted over and introduced himself to Stadler.

"Hey, you're just the guy I want to see. I'm Ray Scapinello."

"Yeah, I know who you are," the Walrus replied.

"You must have a lot of golf clubs hanging around your house," Scampy started.

"Why?"

"Well, I collect stuff," Scampy continued, "and I'm thinking I'd like to trade you my jersey for a golf club you've actually done something with."

"Okay, you've got a deal," Stadler came back.

"Like a putter, driver, something like that," Scampy clarified.

"Okay."

"Are you going to Montreal?" Scampy queried.

"Yep."

"I've got Game Five there, so I'll see you there," Scampy concluded.

"I'll talk to you there," Stadler said.

On the day of Game Five, the two ran into one another in the lobby of the Sheraton and exchanged brief pleasantries, but they didn't discuss the item swap again. Stadler talked about heading to New Jersey to compete in the US Open later in the week, while Scampy was thinking of the game that night, and went on about his business.

"So the game is over, Montreal wins the Cup," Scampy remembers. "I just get in the dressing room and there's a knock at the door. It's the guard."

"Ray!" the security man calls out.

"Yeah."

"Craig Stadler's here to see you."

So Scampy went to the door. "Hey Craig, what can I do for you?" he said pleasantly, momentarily forgetting about the swap.

"I'm here for your jersey."

"Well, it kind of stinks. If you give me your address, I can send it to you."

"No, I want it now," the Walrus stated.

"Okay," Scampy agreed. He took off the jersey, autographed it, and said with a smile, "If you don't send me a club, I'm gonna haunt you 'til the day I die, ha ha."

"I will, I will," Stadler came back. "Thank you, Ray. Take care."

A week later, while golfing in Guelph, Scampy received a call from his wife, Maureen, saying that a man from Golf House at Glen Abbey in Oakville had called. Scampy hurried home and returned the call.

"Hey Ray, I've got something here from Craig Stadler. He gave it to me at the US Open, and he wanted me to give it to you. I'll send it to you," said the local pro on the other end.

"No, no, you're not sending me nothing," Scampy said. "I'll be down within the hour."

Ray grabbed his son, Ryan, and jumped in his Corvette, driving about fifty kilometers to Glen Abbey. The two hustled into the office at Golf House and for fifteen minutes listened to the pro talk hockey.

"Ryan and I are all excited about the Stadler gift, so we're getting antsy standing there talking," Scampy explains. Finally the pro hands Scampy a sand wedge with a note attached.

Ray, this is the club that helped me win the 1984 Masters, hope you enjoy. Your friend, Craig Stadler

"I didn't save the note. I kick my ass to this day for not saving it."

Scampy had the sand wedge that helped Stadler win the Masters in a playoff.

On the way out of Glen Abbey, the 10th hole sits on the right-hand side, with the 11th tee on the left. Scampy stopped the car on the road, grabbed two golf balls out of a bag in his car and went over to the 11th hole, a looong par four that drops from a cliff off the tee. Even if he drilled the sand wedge, he couldn't get it to the fairway.

"Let's hit this sand wedge," Scampy said like a kid at Christmas.

He skulled his shot right into a bush. Ryan hit a nice, straight wedge shot down towards the fairway.

"It was great," Scampy declares.

CHAPTER 7

∽

Had Stadler been sitting in the stands at a game during the last few seasons, Scampy wouldn't have seen him, and chances are he wouldn't have met him.

"It all changed for standby officials a few years ago," Scampy explains. "Those were the days when we didn't have to sit in the dressing room like we do now. If you're standby now you have to sit in the room. You're supposed to have your skates on in case someone gets injured."

The change was precipitated almost a decade ago during a playoff game in Toronto when Pat Dapuzzo suffered an injury. Ron Asselstine was the standby, but instead of going down and getting dressed, he went down to see how Pat was doing in the medical room. Dapuzzo picked up ten or twelve stitches while Asselstine watched.

"Meanwhile, Jim Gregory from the League had to hunt Ron down to get him dressed," Scampy recalls. "It was such a long delay; [Commissioner Gary] Bettman got more than a little ticked off." Bettman declared it would never happen again, and it was the end of the free-to-loiter era.

∽

The free time while on standby came in handy. Scampy remembers that once, prior to the change, standby referee Paul Stewart was trying to do his working cohorts a favor.

"At a playoff game in LA, Paul was wandering around when he ran into Jack Nicholson in a private VIP box," Scampy recalls. "Paul's maybe the most social guy you'd meet in your life, a super-social guy, so he figured he'd do us a favor and have Nicholson come down and visit us."

"My name's Paul Stewart. I'm a referee in the NHL," he said to the movie star. "Would you like to come down and meet the guys?"

Jack Nicholson responded, "Now, why would I want to do something like that?"

Scampy remembers meeting Phil Mickelson, Bob Costas, Gary McCord, and Tom Pertzer during the Colorado/Florida finals in 1996. They were involved in the Doral Open in south Florida at the time and were nice enough to stop by and say hello to the officials.

"Our security guy asked Jack Nicklaus to come down but he wouldn't," Scampy remembers. "We had a couple days off, so the next day Ron Asselstine and I decided to go to the Doral Open. We were walking around and we hear Pertzer being introduced on the first tee. It must have been a Thursday round because there weren't that many people around. We watched Pertzer hit off the first tee and he just pipelined it right down the center. So Ron and I were walking down the right-hand side of the fairway, obviously outside the ropes, as Pertzer was walking down the fairway. Suddenly, he spots us ... he turned, walked across the fairway, across the rough, and came and shook our hands. He walked back, hit his second shot, and made par. We followed him for another hole or two and moved on. No pressure."

~

It's believed hockey players make good golfers because the mechanics of shooting a puck and swinging a golf club are similar. Or, it may just be the fact that hockey players have a lot of time off during the summer months to practice.

Or it's the timing, the precise hand-eye coordination that is involved in both activities. If the latter is the case, then Stan Mikita must be one hell of a golfer. Scampy says Mikita's hand-eye reactions were the best he's ever seen, and therefore Mikita was probably the best face-off man he's ever seen. Scampy should know; he's dropped the puck a couple hundred thousand times.

"Stan Mikita—an incredible face-off man—I don't know what it was, but you couldn't beat him," Scampy states. "And Stan was a tough guy to get along with on the ice; he didn't muck about. A real competitor, he didn't mind telling you what he thought of your work."

~

Lately for Scampy, Kris Draper stands out as a draw man. He hides his cheating well.

"Guys will cheat as much as you allow them," Scampy says. "In the end, they're just good at what they do."

Face-off moves are repeated and practiced, and the hand-eye tricks are incredible. Teams practice face-offs on occasion; centermen work on it in training camp. Cheating involves lunging early, or pivoting one's feet or turning sideways to gain unfair balance and leverage. Nowadays, linesmen, for the most part, make sure the centers are lined up square behind the lines and that the road team center puts his stick down first, as required.

"They look at my idiosyncrasies," Scampy points out with admiration. "Do I move my hand up before I drop the puck down? I do. I think most linesmen move their hands up just a bit before they drop the puck. Do I move my thumb before I drop the puck? I don't, but some do, and the players pick up on stuff like that. The really good ones know enough to start their action right away; they're just great at what they do. They know me better than I know myself when it comes to dropping the puck; they're looking at things I probably don't even realize."

It's all about looking for tendencies, like in a poker game, but instead of winning money you win puck possession. NHL centermen know every linesman, and they know how much cheating they can get away with, who's going to throw them out quick, or who will put up with a lot.

Statistically, Yanic Perreault, now of the Nashville Predators, is the guy who has recently "cheated" the best out of everyone. He's led face-off statistics in the NHL the last few years.

"He's a wonderful centerman," Scampy says, "Nice guy, Yanic, very nice kid."

Joel Otto was a great centerman according to Scampy, and of the superstars, Mario Lemieux stands out.

"Mario! Oh jeez, he's good," Scampy smiles. "Mario wouldn't even try to cheat. He just puts his stick down like it's a peewee house game, and he just snaps it back, snaps it forward, can do anything he wants with it. Gee whiz, unbelievably good.

"Gretzky I wouldn't call a dominant draw guy," Scampy continues, "but he's not going to be taking your biggest draws. Messier was very good at it. Eric Lindros, another good one—strong, strong on the puck. He could move your stick and you couldn't get it back where you wanted it."

CHAPTER 7

~

Lindros actually owns a house in Ontario's cottage country, around the corner from where the Scapinellos rent every summer. An avid fisherman, Lindros often motors or drifts in the bay near Scampy's cottage while fishing for muskie.

"He found out we lived there, and he'd occasionally stop by and have a chat. He's a real gentleman," Scampy points out. Meanwhile, Ryan Scapinello has spent his last few summers at the cottage, training for college hockey.

"So," Scampy starts, "Ryan finished running one day, and happened upon Eric during a fishing visit. Eric asked him where he trained. Ryan said he ran the roads, did whatever he could, wherever. Eric said, 'You can come use my gym at the boathouse. Tie your boat off, it's open, go in there, and do what you want.'"

For three or four summers, Ryan would take the boat over, work out for an hour, and leave. In the summer of 2002, Ryan worked out with Eric almost every day. As Scampy puts it, Eric treated him like royalty. He'd prepare Ryan healthy, solid meals and take him back to the boathouse and guide him through workouts.

"So, I'm doing a game in Ottawa one night," Scampy continues, "and Eric was beating Radek Bonk on every face-off, beating him like a rented mule every time."

The next day, Scampy went home, and then drove to Pittsburgh. As was his custom, Scampy would drive to a regional destination, rather than fly, the night before game night. On this occasion, the Penguins were hosting

Ottawa. Scampy woke up early in the morning, and headed to the rink to casually watch a morning skate or two. The Penguins were taking their team picture that day, so Scampy decided to visit the trainer in the Ottawa dressing room. As he sat there chatting, about an hour before Ottawa would take the ice, Radek Bonk walked by in his underwear.

"Say Radek," Scampy said with a raised voice, "that Lindros beat you on EVERY face-off the other night."

"Yeah," answered Bonk, "You were throwing it right between his legs."

"Yeah, well, I was doing that because he lets my son, Ryan, work out at his gym at his cottage during the summer," Scampy declared with a smile.

"Well, if he comes to the Czech Republic, he can use my gym," Bonk retorted.

About a month later, Scampy was in Madison Square Garden doing a game, Ottawa at New York. During the first period, the Rangers came out over the blue line and an errant pass ended up hopping onto the Ottawa bench.

"So I go to the spot where I thought the face-off was and I just stand there and I get a puck from the other linesman," Scampy recalls. "While I stood there, waiting for the Rangers to finish a line change, Lindros skates over."

"Scamp, it was shot from there," Lindros said while pointing.

"Oh, okay," Scampy says. "No big deal." So Scampy shuffled about four feet to the spot where Eric had pointed.

Radek Bonk, who had been circling around, waiting for the draw, asked, "Where are you going?"

Scampy side-stepped back over and said, "Well, Eric says it should be there."

Bonk says, "Oh yeah, the guy with the cottage."

"Right," Scampy answered with a laugh.

~

Obviously, most face-offs don't come with this much history behind them. Nor do most come with any banter at all. In fact, as the NHL and its player numbers have grown, it's been tougher for officials to establish a rapport with players. The game is not as personal as it used to be; a certain level of familiarity is gone. The recent addition of the hurry-up face-off, where the teams have to be ready to go in fifteen seconds even when they're changing lines, has also helped kill dialogue.

"I pride myself on getting along with most guys," Scampy says. "When I didn't have that rapport is back when I first started. I mean, the seventies Canadiens, I didn't have much going with them. I'd just watch them fly around. I was young, I didn't speak much French, and I was kind of the guy still being broken in.

"I do remember being in Montreal once when Lafleur was going in on pretty much a clean breakaway, and he got hauled down," Scampy continues. "I was looking for Wicksy's arm to come up and it didn't. Lafleur slid into the corner, the whistle went a few moments later, and here come the Canadiens off the bench. Lafleur didn't say a word. He had an army of teammates over there in Wicksy's face wondering what the hell was going on."

"Where's the penalty shot, blah blah blah," Scampy mimics a gang. "I looked over at the bench and Lafleur had just cruised over and sat down—a general letting his troops handle the disagreement for him. He wouldn't come and whine about a hook or a hold or a penalty shot, ever, ever. Never said a word."

Of the French-Canadian superstars, Mario Lemieux handled himself in a similar fashion for the most part: not a real talkative guy, and very respectful.

He and Lafleur probably both learned from the example set by Jean Beliveau, a player who exuded class and level-headedness as a Montreal leader and captain during the fifties and sixties.

"I understand Jean Beliveau was unreal," Scampy points out. "What a guy. Rarely if ever said anything to a referee or linesman, and if he did, you'd listen. If he said you missed a call, there was a pretty damn good chance you missed it. He'd never raised his voice or tried to get personal."

Another well-respected captain, Steve Yzerman, occasionally runs into Scampy off the ice. They both spend time on the same lake during the summer.

"I'm on the east side of the lake where I rent a humble abode," Scampy says. "Yzerman's is across the way, and it's a beautiful new place he had built. A couple years ago, my vacation was finished up there, but Maureen and I wanted to go up one more time in September for one last chance to water ski."

Just prior to the trip, Scampy was doing an exhibition game in Detroit, so during a lull in the game he asked Yzerman about the house.

"It's almost done, Scamp," Yzerman said.

"Hey, you know, I'm going up there next week. Do you mind if I just pull up to your dock, walk around, and check out the project?" Scampy asked.

"Well, Scamp, I'd prefer not having any riffraff walking around out there," Yzerman said, with no attempt to keep a straight face.

"He's class on and off the ice," Scampy says. "We'll run into him every once in a while up north. A real gentleman. He'll stand the whole time he's talking to Maureen, that kind of thing. A shy, polite man." Scampy remembers the first time he met Mr. and Mrs. Yzerman together.

"Your husband yells at me *all* the time," Scampy quipped.

"Oh, c'mon Scamp, I don't yell at you that much," Stevie Y. responded, slightly embarrassed.

Also on Scampy's respect list are two gentlemen that stand out: Grant Ledyard, and Darren McCarty, a former Red Wing teammate of Yzerman's.

"Those two strike me as the top of the heap in terms of class guys," Scampy says, "and McCarty's always there to offer you a cold drink during a TV timeout."

Of the meaningful banter that actually takes place between officials and participants these days, most goes on during the television time-outs, and even then, conversations don't last very long. On one occasion, Scampy remembers a series of chats with a most unexpected source, Maple

Leafs goaltender Eddie Belfour. Belfour is well known for being intensely focused during game days. In fact, it's likely that those close to Belfour walk on eggshells around the netminder near game time, as he won't likely talk to anyone before a match.

The exception came in 2002 when during a break on the ice Eddie asked Scampy for his officials jersey. Apparently, Belfour's son really liked watching Scampy.

"Absolutely, I'll autograph it and send it down," Scampy told him, which he did right after the game.

The next game in Toronto, Belfour made a point of skating over right before the action started and thanking Scampy for the jersey.

"Thank you so much for the jersey," Eddie the Eagle said profusely.

"Oh, you're very welcome," Scampy said with smile. He was a little surprised, not by the appreciation, but by the timing.

The following season, Scampy wanted Belfour's goalie stick for a neighbor kid who lives across the street from him. The boy's mom had told Scampy how much her son, Michael, loved Eddie. Scampy was hoping to get the stick in time for Christmas 2003.

"I started by asking Tank, broadcaster Joe Bowen's son, who helps out with the Leafs' equipment, to help me get a stick," Scampy recalls. "I tried to get him to ask before the game."

Tank often brought drinks, towels, and supplies to the officials' dressing room.

"Hey Tank, can you ask Belfour for a stick tonight, have him autograph it to Michael?" Scampy asked.

Tank was superstitious and a little petrified. "I'm not talking to him before he heads out," he said.

"C'mon, just go there and tell him I need the damn stick," Scampy urged.

"No way, man. Not me," Tank answered.

So Scampy skated out onto the ice, waited for the right moment before the game started, and scooted by the net.

"Hey Ed, any chance I could get a stick from you?"

"Oh, sure Scamp. For you?" Belfour answered.

"No, I need it for my neighbor. His name's Michael."

"Okay Scamp." After the game, Belfour brought the stick down to the officials' room to make sure Scampy received it.

"This, from a guy who's pretty much the closest thing to a modern-day Bobby Clark in terms of his on-ice demeanor," Scampy says.

When Scampy gave Michael's mom the stick to pass on to her son, tears welled up in her eyes. She was so happy and appreciative that she stood in her garage and cried.

"That was really nice of Eddie. And I'll tell you what, as for his intensity most of the time, I don't hold that against him. It's a business and he's got a job to do. I respect the fact that everyone has their own way of taking care of business."

∾

The memorabilia-collecting phenomena is a two-way street. Just like a percentage of fans and officials, the players themselves also have a collecting itch they like to scratch.

Scampy probably signed and gave away about six or seven of his sweaters a season, mostly as charitable contributions but sometimes to players. His first two jerseys from the League were free, but each subsequent replacement cost him about thirty or forty bucks a piece.

"In terms of players, Bob Probert asked me for my jersey one time. Domi has one, and Ray Bourque as well," Scampy points out.

Andy Van Hellemond, during his tenure as Director of Officiating, discouraged the bartering and collecting.

"Mainly for that reason," linesman Scott Driscoll says, "I'll barter for things that are more away from hockey, like a number 68 NBA official's jersey, or an umpire's jacket."

Driscoll *did* pick up a Dwayne Roloson autographed stick when he worked the All-Star Game in 2004. Roloson, whose best childhood friend played university hockey with Driscoll, autographed it for Scott's eight-year-old son.

"Scampy's hilarious. I know he gives most of his stuff to charity, but he was relentless. I'm still not sure if he was completely serious in Buffalo once when Rollie was backing up Dominic Hasek. Scampy said to Hasek, 'Hey, see if you can get a pair of Dwayne Roloson's goalie pads. He's not using them.'" Scampy's requests became a running topic of conversation and fun around NHL rinks, and his memorabilia collecting became legendary.

"The Hall of Fame has to call Scampy to get him to loan them stuff sometimes," says Rip Simonick, the Buffalo equipment guy.

During his years in the League, former NHL referee Mark Faucette earned renown for his sketches and cartoons. One of his best zingers showed Scampy after the closing of Maple Leaf Gardens, driving Toronto's Zamboni back home to Guelph.

"Oh man, he's relentless," referee Paul Devorski claims. "With Scampy it was an ongoing joke. After a game in Buffalo, Scampy's talking to Rip, and all of a sudden he's walking out with elbow pads, shin pads, and shoulder pads. You know, you'd see him do it there, then you'd see him do it in another arena."

One night, Devorski playfully confronted him.

"Scampy, how much frickin' equipment does your boy need?" Devo asked.

"You know, his team changes colors every year." Scampy shot back, laughing.

"Holy shit, he had sticks, everything," Devo remembers.

"Most of the stuff I got was sticks," Scampy admits. "How the hell I managed to lug those things around, I don't know."

"Anything that was free and wasn't nailed down was his," adds former linesman cohort Leon Stickle. "He was a great guy for collecting things as he went around, and we always joked about him selling memorabilia in the Guelph square for more than retail. There was a sporting goods store near the Guelph Memorial Gardens, and Scampy had more sporting goods for sale than they did."

"He was definitely a barterer," confirms linesman Brad Kovachik. "A lot of people joked about him being cheap, himself included, but one thing many don't realize about Ray is how much he does for charity. A lot of what he collects goes to useful causes."

⁓

Early in his career during a visit to Boston, Scampy went to a Red Sox game and was invited into the dugout by manager Don Zimmer. After he visited with Carl Yastrzemski for a while, Yaz gave Scampy an autographed bat. Scampy stored the bat in his office. One day the kids in the neighborhood were playing baseball up the road and needed a bat. They came by Scampy's house but unfortunately Ray wasn't home.

"Hi, Mrs. Scapinello," they said. "Do you have a baseball bat we could use?"

"Hmmm, well, I know there's one in Ray's office," Maureen answered. She fetched it and gave it to the kids, who immediately took it to the top of the street and hit baseballs and stones down the hill with it.

"In Maureen's defense," Scampy says, "she did ask them to bring it back when they were done with it."

⁓

In terms of ultimate bartering, linesman Wayne Bonney may be the one-time champion. During a transaction that took several years, crossed the continent, and involved multiple trades, Bonney pulled off a whopper.

CHAPTER 7

"When I lived in Montreal, I had a friend, [we'll call him] Jerry, who owned a marble company," Bonney relates as background to what's to come. "When Mario Lemieux retired the first time, he had his final game in Montreal, and he gave the jersey he wore that night to Phil Schroeder, who did scheduling for the NHL. Phil kept the sweater at his house."

In the off-season, Bonney installed sprinkler systems, and at one point he installed one for Phil. For a decent-size house like the one Schroeder owned, the sprinkler job would normally cost about two to three thousand dollars.

"How much?" Phil asked.

"Well, if you can get me a Mario Lemieux jersey, I'll do it for nothing," Bonney answered after secretly admiring the number 66 hanging on the wall. Phil agreed and gave Bonney the jersey from the Montreal game.

Fast-forward to years later, with Bonney and his wife relocated to the west coast.

"I had since moved to Seattle in 1993 and was putting marble in my three bathrooms in our new house," Bonney recalls. "My wife went to Toronto to order marble. She picked it out from Jerry's store there—Jerry, the friend we knew from Montreal."

When Bonney heard the prices, he winced but agreed to make the purchase. He also jumped on the phone to make Jerry a proposal and hopefully ease the pain.

"I'll give you a Mario Lemieux jersey, signed, for your son, for some consideration on the marble," Bonney offered. Jerry thought that sounded pretty good, but that was it—the proposal just hung there. Jerry went ahead and shipped out all of the marble, twelve to fifteen thousand dollars worth (retail) to Seattle. It cost seventeen hundred bucks just to ship it.

"Wayne, what understanding did you have on this marble and the Mario Lemieux sweater?" Jerry asked him after sending the invoice.

"Well, I thought you were going to give me all of the marble for the Lemieux sweater, but I thought you were f——ing nuts," Bonney laughed.

"Yeah, well, I can't do that. I can't give you twelve grand worth of marble for a jersey," Jerry came back.

"Well, yeah, I thought you were a bit nuts," Bonney said. "I'm more than fair. What do you want to do?"

"Actually, I can get away with giving you the marble, but I can't get away from the seventeen hundred dollars in shipping," Jerry came back. "Can you pay it?"

"I'll send you a check tomorrow," Bonney replied. Bonney had his marble. What a deal—the envy of short, bald linesmen everywhere.

⁓

Hockey paraphernalia collecting carries a sense of the same boys-will-be-boys concept that applies to practical joking. Of course, in this case, it seems more like fanaticism. Although they don't worship certain players like some fans do, the officials are indeed fans in their own way. And for as long as there have been fans and players, the fans have wanted a *piece* of the players. It's simply part of the sport, and for hockey supporters, which officials are, it's part of the game's rich history. Fortunately for Scampy and his pals, linesmen have a much easier time getting material from players than referees do. The linesmen make peace for the most part, while the referees, in the eyes of players, cause problems, make stupid calls, and piss people off.

Case in point: Paul Devorski.

"I remember one night I said to Eric Lindros, 'Hey Eric, I have a picture I'd like you to sign.' I brought it myself—no one was giving it to me—and wouldn't you know, first five minutes of the game, I give him an instigator penalty and toss him, so I felt like complete crap going down there after the game," says Devorski. "It's uncomfortable for referees. I mean maybe, if you're walking out after a game, and you run into a guy ... like Joe Sakic. He's such a class guy. If you saw him after the game in the tunnel, you might say, 'Hey Joe, will you sign this for my buddy?'"

Linesman Mark Pare, not one overly enthused about memorabilia or autograph acquisition, experienced a situation very much along those lines.

"Pittsburgh was visiting Detroit," Pare says. "My family had made the trip over with me, and we stopped by the rink during the skates to say hello to Al Sobotka [the ice man, rink operations man, and the octopus man for many years in Motown]. As we're walking in, Mario Lemieux, Ron Francis, Bryan Trottier, and Kevin Stevens are walking out. My daughter wanted Lemieux's autograph."

"No, c'mon, let the guys be," Pare first responded.

"Let her get one," his wife urged. "They're not doing anything."

So Pare's daughter, Lindsay, with her broken arm in a cast, approached and politely asked Lemieux for his signature. Lindsay only had a ballpoint pen, but Mario pulled out a marker and signed her plaster.

"She was thrilled," Pare says. "She showed that cast to all of her friends, even after she had it removed. It started to reek a little bit, but she still has it in her closet."

Pare's desire to allow the players their space off the ice doesn't mean he lacks an appreciation for their star power, or their world-class abilities.

"Sometimes you see guys do things and you're like 'Wow,'" Pare declares. "You can't really be a fan and pay attention to the moves so much—you have to do your job—but sometimes you see things you can't believe. Gretzky was amazing, obviously. He'd leave you talking to yourself. He was trapped in the corner once, playing for the Rangers in his last year. Nashville had two guys in front of their net, cheating towards him. He was being pressed, so he fired the puck off the side of the net. It caromed perfectly in front to Kevin Stevens and he rapped it in. It wasn't dumb luck, he planned it, and I was standing on the ice thinking, 'That was awesome.'"

"Gretzky, Joe Sakic, and Yzerman are very kind, class guys," Pare concludes. "I haven't met a bad hockey guy off the ice. They leave the game on the ice."

This down-to-earth mentality is what brings the hockey community together as one. Hockey people generally like other hockey people regardless of how much they earn or what their role is, simply because they're involved in the game. Media members who cover all of the major sports, whether they prefer hockey or not, will often say, "Hockey players are the easiest and best to deal with." It's universal. Part of this is the simple rural Canadian and American roots of many of the players over the decades, part of it is the stringent concept that team comes first, and part of it is the general lack of "bling bling" and the positive work ethic that comes from both.

It's not cool or generally accepted to be a selfish, loud, extroverted jackass in hockey, as is often accepted and even promoted in baseball, football, or hoops. Does this keep a certain element of the North American mainstream disinterested in the game, or prevent an element of promotion? Maybe, but that's just fine. Scampy would rather talk about good guys, in a great game.

"Ray Bourque is another real class act," points out Scampy. "He went out on top. I remember the year he won the Cup in Colorado. We were working the playoffs there.

"On an off-night, we're at a very nice restaurant, steak restaurant. Chris Drury and Bourque were having dinner in a back room. On his way out, Ray came by and sat down by us," Scampy continues. "It was graduation night for some high school students, and kids were coming over one after the other asking for his autograph. He's a real gentleman. He signed them all."

"Hey, my daughter's out there tonight—you treat these ladies with the utmost respect," Bourque told the teenagers.

"Yes, Mr. Bourque," the boys answered.

"He finished chatting with us, went back to say good-bye to Drury, and three or four minutes later he walked out and waved goodbye to us," Scampy says. "We had had steak, a bottle of wine, full courses, real nice meal. We're done and we ask the waiter for the bill."

"Mr. Bourque picked up your bill," the waiter told the officials.

"Mr. Bourque did?" they questioned.

"Yes," came the reply.

"Well, give us the ballpark so we can take care of a nice gratuity," Scampy posed.

"That won't be necessary. Mr. Bourque took care of it. Take your time, gentlemen. You're all set whenever you're ready to go."

Keep in mind, class acts or acts of generosity are not going to garner favor with the officials. Nor is any childhood affiliation with a favorite team or player.

"Could you imagine," wonders Scampy, "how long an official would last if he made preferential calls based on his favorite team? He wouldn't last ten minutes. There's none of that. In fact, it would be impossible. No one has time on an offside to check a jersey number and say, 'Oh yeah, that's such and such. I think I'll let this one go.' Never once in my thirty-three years did I see it. It's just not gonna happen."

As it relates to Scampy's childhood favorites, he didn't have any.

CHAPTER 7

"I know it sounds a bit odd, but I really never had a favorite team or player," he says. "Don't ask me why. Around here in Guelph, they bleed blue and white, but for whatever reason I never got caught up in it."

As for the best players he's ever seen, Scampy says you'd probably have to hold a gun to his head.

"I guess I'd say Gretzky, and for goalies I'd have to say Roy," Scampy points out. "But I mean, I was on the ice with Ken Dryden, Mario Lemieux, so how can I pick one or two? I'm infatuated with how great they are and being on the ice with them, but it's really impossible to narrow it down."

Bottom line? Scampy loves the great players, the game itself, and practically everyone in his extensive hockey family.

CHAPTER 8

NHL Evolutions

Scampy provided a great lesson to the younger guys. You're in the NHL—there are no shortcuts anymore. You have to be ready to go game after game after game. It doesn't matter what you did last night. It's a lesson for all of us. He was a pro, yet no one had more fun.
—Rob Shick, veteran NHL referee

Many things have changed in the NHL since Scampy entered the League three and a half decades ago. The most obvious stands out every time a veteran official enters a building: It's the buildings themselves. For the most part, the personality of the individual arenas in each town has been lost.

"I used to love going to the Forum," Scampy says, "always a thrill. After it was freshly flooded, I used to walk around the ice in Montreal ... there'd be TV lights all over.

"We used to walk down a corridor, take a left-hand turn where the Zamboni came out, the gates would be open, and we'd step down onto the ice and buzz around five or six times before the players came out. I'd check the nets, cruise, and breathe in the ambience."

Scampy remembers Claude Mouton, who used to be the public address announcer at the Forum, and for the Expos baseball team.

"He'd always introduce John Boccabella, an Expos player, by saying, 'Jooohhnnn Bocc!-a-beelllll-aaaaaaaa.' So he started doing something like that for me. He'd always wait until we came on the ice to introduce us. Even if we were late for some reason, he'd wait and do the introductions."

Scampy imitates Mouton: "Referee Terry Gregson, the judge de line, Gerard Gau-tieerr, and Senor Raymondo Scamp!-a-neelllllooooooooo ... "

"The fans would cheer and I'd skate by and smile at Claude," Scampy concludes fondly.

"The Forum was relatively quiet, and in Toronto, they'd sit on their hands," reflects long-time ref Wally Harris. "Detroit, New York, and Boston could get pretty raucous, but nothing came close to Chicago Stadium. The fans, the noise, the organ, the horn ... there was nothing like it."

"Chicago was unbelievable," concurs retired linesman Leon Stickle. "Wayne Mesmer sang the anthem, but you couldn't hear him. You could feel the drone of the organ, but you couldn't hear the sound; the fans just rocked the place. I loved the old buildings. I'm glad I got to work in that era with the old buildings."

Stickle requested, and was granted, his last game at Maple Leaf Gardens. The Leafs hosted the Calgary Flames, with both teams out of the playoffs. Stickle didn't work the post season his final year, ensuring that the Milton, Ontario native's last effort would be in Toronto. As last games go, however, it was a finale of a different sort that truly stands out for Stickle.

"I worked, I believe with Gerard Gautier, the last game played at the Montreal Forum. I saw them pass the torch between the captains, the old-timers. The Dallas Stars played the last game there, so [then Stars GM and former Hab] Bob Gainey could get involved heavily. It was like a three-day event. It was amazing. And the sad thing is, that place could have supported hockey for another twenty years.

"The old Olympia in Detroit was a neat building," Stickle continues, "but probably the most inconvenient place to work, with tight quarters, and you'd come out through a tunnel where the fans were all over you. Howe had played there, Delvecchio ... great atmosphere."

Long before he was an NHL linesman, Mark Pare, who grew up across the border in Ontario, remembers the Red Wings for a different reason.

"People in Windsor hated the Red Wings back in the late sixties and seventies because they blacked out *Hockey Night in Canada* to make sure the fans would either go to or watch the Wings games," Pare remembers. "Ted Lindsay came along in 1977 and said the Wings would never black out *Hockey Night in Canada* again." ("Terrible Ted's" marketing slogan at the time was "Aggressive Hockey Is Back in Town.") Fans started to like them again, and of course, they eventually started to get better.

~

As mentioned, for cost reasons, an official will handle most of his games in one region, when back during early post-expansion, refs and linesmen would travel all over the continent handling games night to night.

"There are officials living all over the continent now, and they work in their own areas for the most part," Scampy reiterates. "There used to be a lot less of us, and we'd go to California one day, then maybe New York a couple of days later. We never partnered. We might work together for two or three games in an area, but then we'd go our own way."

Now, officials will rotate continuously, but they'll end up working with the limited number of guys in their own region quite often.

Before, in the smaller league, with fewer officials on hand during the one-referee era, it meant the camaraderie ran deep throughout the entire staff.

"It might sound like bullshit," Scampy states, "but the guys got along very well, and they still do. It's very rare, if at all, to hear of a pissing match for any reason. I can't remember any. We get along great, and it's a close-knit bunch of guys for the most part."

The nature of the job keeps officials tight. Empathy runs deep over the course of a season and also night to night, because crazy shit and controversy happens to all of them.

"We're a close-knit group when we're together, but not really when we're not working," Scampy admits. "I worked a ton of games with Gord Broseker over the years, big ones, but now we never talk. Guys have tried to reach Gord since he retired and he generally doesn't call guys back."

Scampy will occasionally run into some of the local guys, since Ron Asselstine is a Guelphite, as is Andy Van Hellemond, Willie Norris, and Bill McCreary.

"I do chat with Billy a lot, and I'm close to his family, but when we're home in the summer, we're usually all off doing our own thing," Scampy says. "We're not barbecuing together. I never see them. I'm off in my own little world and they're doing their own thing."

Like the other Guelphites in the NHL officiating ranks, McCreary came up through the OHA, an association with a rich officiating tradition.

"Guelph was considered one of the stronger organizations in the country," Mac points out, "with a lot of hard work in administration and on-ice. I was fortunate to work with a lot of great people that went on to various levels. You could really develop if you had skills and a hockey background. Lou Masho, Bill Devorski, Mel McPhee—all of those guys were [from] Guelph," says McCreary, "with Jack Mann, Jack McKinnon, and Harry Green working on rules and deportment. I remember Evo Parasoto; he worked on the ice into his sixties."

Guelph is, of course, in Ontario, and few people represent Ontario hockey and Ontario hockey officiating more than Jim Gregory. He's been around the NHL for parts of five decades.

"I was around when Scampy first started," Gregory says. "There aren't many of us that can say that. I was already working with the Leafs. Before that, when he worked in the OHL, I was coaching junior hockey. So, I've known Scampy a long time, and I've seen a lot of good officials come through. I went into officiating in 1982, after being fired by the Leafs in '79, and then after running the NHL's Central Scouting Bureau. I was made Vice President of Hockey Operations in 1982. I used to have officials work at our Haliburton Hockey Haven, which I owned for a while.

"Of course, of all the Ontario guys, Scampy's the most unbelievable. I sometimes wonder if it's possible he really worked all of those games, and he did," Gregory marvels. "You'd be hard-pressed to find people that don't have high praise for him. He rarely, rarely got into confrontations with coaches or managers, he handled banter beautifully, and he kept players and benches informed. He did lots of little things that other young officials have learned from."

Over time, young officials become veterans, and through yet another tradition, they earn opportunities.

"Once you're around a while, usually ten years, they'll throw your name in there for the All-Star Game," says ref Paul Devorski, "and once you get to your first All-Star Game, a referee can get autographs," points out Devo. "The players let you go in the room, you can take your son [and daughter, if you have one] in the room. I worked the game in Tampa Bay. You usually work very few All-Star Games, especially now, with so many officials."

By the way, generally out of old-fashioned courtesy, wives of any active hockey participants rarely, if ever, enter a dressing room, and young daughters may only get a glimpse inside once it's assured everyone is dressed.

Scampy worked All-Star Games in Detroit, New Jersey, Toronto, and also the two-game Rendez-Vouz Series in 1987.

CHAPTER 8

As a substitute for the regular NHL All-Star Game, the Rendez-Vouz event pitted NHL All-Stars against the Soviet National Team, considered that year to be one of the best international teams ever. The NHL won Game One 4–3, while the Russians came back to win Game Two 5–3.

Other plum assignments involve international travel, and are awarded mostly on merit. Brad Kovachik was thrilled to work the 2004 World Cup in Sweden and Finland.

"I was surprised and honored," he says. "Sixteen of us were chosen for it. For us to go overseas and represent the officials was an honor. The hockey scene was different over there—a more festive atmosphere. I'd like to see everyone get a chance to see something like that in their careers."

Linesman Mark Pare visited the same two countries the previous year, working Toronto's exhibition games during the Maple Leafs' overseas training camp.

"Sweden was a beautiful place," Pare says, "although we really only saw Stockholm. The bizarre thing was, there was a funeral for a Swedish foreign minister while we were there … this lady who was murdered. There was lots of security, and the funeral kind of cast a pall over the games a bit; she was a very popular politician. Some nut stabbed her at the entrance to one of the largest department stores in Sweden. Anyway, we were treated very well there; we stayed in the same hotel as the Leafs."

Pare spent an entire week in Sweden and Finland with fellow officials Terry Gregson, Don Van Massenhoven, and Dan McCourt. In 1998, Pare also worked exhibition games between Montreal and Tampa Bay in Austria.

Domestic gigs can also be of special interest.

"I worked an outdoor game in Vegas once," remembers ref Rob Shick. "Rangers/Kings exhibition, and Caesar drove the Zamboni. Another cool one was the time Queen Elizabeth attended the game in Vancouver. Gretzky was at that one, too."

Shick's officiating skills developed out west, where he grew up. He used to work in the Western Canada Hockey League.

"There were only eleven NHL refs on staff when I was hired," Shick says. "I first started by doing thirty-five hand-picked games, and then was standby in the playoffs." Because of a ref's decision to retire, he got a last-minute call from John McCauley to work the playoffs in 1987, and he's made every post season since.

~

Background and geography meant nothing to the officials during the NHL lockout. Many of them went to work in "regular" jobs, as car salesmen, in furniture mills, or as laborers. This was due to the fact that as a group, they didn't have lockout pay or insurance.

Obviously during the lockout itself and into 2005, the NHL players' collective bargaining situation garnered a lot of hockey media attention. And although it's never generated as much interest, the NHL officials weren't immune to labor woes of their own. At the same time the players' contract expired in 2004, the officials' contract had expired as well. Unfortunately for them, in their most recent previous negotiation five years prior to the work stoppage, the officials gave up the right to emergency pay during a lockout or strike. During the NHL lockout, not one official received a dime of pay from the League, based on the agreement achieved by League Commissioner Gary Bettman and his boys back in 1999.

Recently, matters have improved. The officials' current deal was signed amicably in April of 2006. The four-year contract doesn't have to worry about strike or lockout arrangements, as it's shorter than the players' agreement. But the refs and linesmen will get pay increases of up to thirty percent over the four years, and they all seem happy with the result and with work conditions.

By the way, under the new deal, all new officials entering the League will have to wear a helmet and visor.

If they weren't leaning that way already, an incident at a Florida Panthers game on November 23, 2005 sealed the deal. Referee Don Van Massenhoven took a deflected ninety-mile-per-hour slap shot right between the eyes. It shattered his orbital bones, cracked his forehead and nose, and pushed his septum right back against his brain. Seven hours of emergency surgery put Van Massenhoven back together again, and seven weeks later he was back on the ice.

"I have seven titanium plates in my head, holding me together," Don says, "and about thirty screws."

Getting back to the summer of 2004, the officials voted not to take any jobs at other levels during the lockout, or to work any game that wasn't for charity or international competition. This was the League's preference as well. The officials overwhelmingly agreed that taking a job away from an up-and-coming official at a lower level wasn't in anyone's best interest. The players jumped to Europe, to the American Hockey League, and even down to the double-A ECHL and Central Leagues. The officials said no; no one was allowed to even drop down to the AHL. It was a pretty solid alliance and impressive fidelity to principle for a group that had a history of never really being that organized.

"Until the late sixties and seventies, the officials didn't even think about having an association. In fact, they were trying to form an association in the late sixties and a lot of the guys weren't interested," former Referee-in-Chief Scotty Morrison remembers.

"Four or five of the senior guys didn't believe in the association. John Ashley, Art Skov, Matt Pavelich, Neil Armstrong, and a couple of others preferred negotiating and talking performance with me directly."

Morrison remembers Joe Kane, a lawyer and former President of the Central Hockey League, pushing for an officials' association that would negotiate all conditions, including travel, pay, and expenses. NHL President Clarence Campbell's initial response was "No way."

"We preferred simply forming an officials' committee, to review all of those matters," Morrison says. "I'd meet with them periodically as a rep of the League. That wasn't good enough for Joe. Camp was in Brantford that year and many of the officials walked out."

Five or six of the dissenters did not.

"We want to talk to you directly, Scotty," they said.

Eventually the organization led by Kane won out, and Campbell and the League recognized the officials as a bargaining unit.

"That was a real harrowing experience, walking out," recalls referee Wally Harris. "I remember Vern Buffy was prominent, and I was actually president of the association the third year we got it started."

"That was 1970, I believe," remembers Scampy. "I wasn't hired yet, but it was the first year I was invited to a camp. I remember showing up in Brantford, walking into the hotel, and some of the officials were walking out."

Eventually, the entire group got back together and decided to crawl before they could walk. Most of their original demands or requests were elementary.

"It still didn't affect contracts immediately—those were still negotiated one-on-one—but everything else was decided as a group," Morrison recalls. "I got a little ticked off at Kane. I worked with him when he ran the CHL. It was a good training ground for officials, and then all of a sudden he's on the other side. He was a good lawyer though; he later became a judge in Toronto."

Maybe it was the taste of irony that bothered Morrison. Before the emergence of the officials' association, he had actually been the one to standardize some of the review and payment procedures with the NHL. When he started, officials were paid on a per-game basis, even in the playoffs, while many of them were only part time.

"I worked with Mr. Campbell to get that standardized and get the guys full time," Morrison says. "We needed consistency and professionalism. Gradually, officiating really became a very fine career for someone who played hockey, wanted to stay in the game, understood the game, and had the mental toughness. I think the tough part has always been traveling and being away from home," Morrison concludes.

"The organization of the officials in terms of a labor group went hand in hand with how the job became more serious," Scampy says. "Not that we didn't always take it seriously … it just became more of a full-time, full-year job. We organized, we started a stricter training schedule year round, and I guess with that we earned more money. The per diem went up, everything, the stakes went up, and the profession became more competitive."

∽

Negotiating issues arise periodically. Prior to joining the NHL ranks in 1990, former ref Stephen Walkom remembers a lot of tension between the non-voting trainees and the regular officials at preseason camp in 1988.

"We were at a chalet in Etobicoke [near the Toronto airport]," Walkom says, "they had just signed a new five-year deal and there was a little dissention. I remember Paul Stewart arranged a putting tournament along the side of the chalet to help break the tension. He felt we were taking ourselves way too seriously."

"I remember the putting tournament. I kept making money hand over fist against Stewy," Scampy laughs. "I kept letting him stroke the putts. He couldn't make 'em. He kept missing this right-to-lefter."

Eventually, the officials settled any differences they might have had and for the most part have been a very cohesive group over the years.

"Absolutely! It's been a tight, strong group on the labor stuff," Scampy agrees.

～

One big change in recent years that spurred a great deal of debate was the full-time institution of the two-referee system in 2000. Scampy prefers the one-man system, but sees the benefits of both.

"The teams knew what was going to be called," Scampy says, referring to the old system. "Whether it was good, bad, or indifferent, they knew Ron Wicks was going to call a game this way; they knew Bill McCreary was going to call a game that way. With two officials, it's a couple of different personalities. The way I look at a hook, and you look at a hook, it may be [one] or it may not be. You call it down in your end, but if it happens down in my end, there's a good chance I'm probably not going to call it, because I don't think it's a hook. The players get confused.

"The game's faster, and I totally agree that one guy can miss stuff behind his back and it's tougher to catch up to the play in certain instances," Scampy continues. "With two guys, one ref is always waiting for the play to come right toward him, and with the video replay, you're never going to miss the most important goals; it'll go to video review. Everything's pretty well covered, I'd say.

"The best thing is," Scampy points out, "it's created a lot of jobs for some guys that may not have had the opportunity to work in the NHL, and I'm happy for them. A lot of people were in favor of the two referees—owners and GMs—but I think some of them have swayed back. I never see it going back to one, though, unless they do that and change the whole format, and give a lot of responsibility back to the linesmen. But then you start getting linesmen substituting their judgment, and then you've got three refs, to a degree."

"My era, it was all one referee," says Leon Stickle. "It just so happens the hockey was better. The regular season pressure was greater than it is now because the games meant more—fewer teams made the playoffs."

"I think having two refs hurts the real strong ref who has a feel for the game, knows the players, and can dictate the flow," points out former coach turned broadcaster Harry Neale. "There's less flow now [speaking before the lockout], and one ref was fine. There were no more complaints than there are now. The good ones saw most of the stuff—Skov, McCauley, Andy Van Hellemond. Part of the art of coaching was knowing the refs. I'd tell the players, 'This ref likes a rough game but don't be stupid.' And I'd know not to speak to Ron Wicks because he'd give me two minutes just for saying hello."

As the man running the officiating department, Bryan Lewis was not only instrumental in instituting the two-man system, he was also the main catalyst behind video goal review a decade prior. Most would agree the video system works, except for Brett Hull's foot-in-the-crease goal to win the Cup for Dallas over Buffalo in 1999.

"That goal all revolved around possession and control," Lewis says, "and we basically wrote out a dissertation on it. That was the end of a two-year experiment with the crease rule, which was implemented because the goalies were getting hounded. It was tough."

For the entire 1998–99 season, if an offensive player had so much as a skate lace in the goalie crease when the puck entered the net, the goal was waved off. In Game Six of the Finals, Hull's skate was in the crease when he scored the Cup-winning goal. The League argued Hull had control of the puck in the crease before his skate entered the crease. This was the one apparent exception to the rule.

"That rule wasn't really clarified," Scampy says. "I remember Don Cherry saying that it would cost a team a Cup or maybe screw up a big game. I guess he was right."

Lewis's history with League officiating runs deep, starting as a referee in the early seventies, followed in 1985 by three years as a supervisor for John McCauley prior to McCauley's death, and then a dozen years running the shop.

"I remember 'pitting my shants,' being out there in the early days with D'Amico and Pavelich," Lewis laughs, "I was out there with hockey history."

Little did he know at the time that he'd eventually help *make* hockey history with all of the officiating innovations.

"We started working on the video replay with Stu Hackel out of the NHL in New York in the late eighties," Lewis says. "He had video connections at Sony. The rest of the officiating business, it remains common sense, which is tough because everything now has to be so letter-perfect. When I started, I think the rulebook was about seventy pages; now it's probably about 270. It's common sense. The toughest part remains leaving home."

Prior to the 2005–06 season, the other biggest officiating controversy in recent times had been the amount of obstruction, hooking, and holding going on around the ice, and the apparent lack of calls.

Despite experiments with early season "crackdowns" on the infractions, the "crackdowns" usually faded away. It all changed this past season. Hooks and holds are being called with great regularity, the game has opened up, and the players are gradually figuring out the new standards, while the officials are trying to stay consistent.

"I think the new rules are great," Scampy says, "The officiating department has been following the new guidelines right from start to finish. Everyone I talk to thinks the games are just wonderful."

Or to paraphrase great Canadiens Captain Jean Beliveau, "It reminds me of when I used to play. We'd use our sticks for shooting, passing, and stick-handling, not for hooking or holding."

"I think the guys are being consistent," Scampy asserts. "And if they're not, they're going to hear about it. The e-mails and conference calls start rolling in from the League office as soon as anyone starts to slip. It's always been that way. We'd get them for face-offs, if they thought things were getting a bit lax. We might get it at a game. A supervisor might come down and say, 'Hey, there were three obstructions in this game that needed to be called. Let's not slack off on that.' Gary Bettman was adamant about that stuff."

"Writers knock us about the way the game used to be called," says ref Bill McCreary. "They don't know shit from shinola. We had well-paced, two-hour-and-seven-minute games before, and they've only gotten better. We must be doing something right, and the players have responded well."

'Every game is viewed at mission control in Toronto," Scampy reminds, "since there's not a supervisor at every game. It's not like in the old days … you'd go to California and everyone would say, 'Oh, you're on vacation out there, a sunburn trip.' Not anymore. Every game is scrutinized— different camera angles—everything is analyzed, and you don't get away with anything. The scrutiny level may have changed, but in terms of actually doing the job, and the responsibilities, they're the same."

Other job responsibilities have been around for a while, like turning in ice and game reports. Officials turn in ice condition and game reports from an unbiased viewpoint after every game.

"We'd rotate who'd do the reports," Scampy says. "On Mondays, the junior ref and linesmen would do the report. On Tuesday games the senior guys would do it. It only takes about ten minutes to jot down some comments.

"Edmonton had incredible ice; Maple Leaf Gardens had terrible ice," Scampy points out. "It was like skating through sand, because [owner Harold] Ballard wouldn't spend the dough to upgrade the systems. Dallas has always had problems because of the heat and humidity down there; the ice would snow up a lot, even with the help of dehumidifiers."

These days, because of more advanced refrigeration systems and ice resurfacing machines that shoot the water down rather than sprinkle it, the ice is getting more consistent around the league.

"Using two machines helps the ice as well," Scampy points out. "With only one machine a few years ago, we'd have to squeegee off the extra water. Now, it's done faster and the ice has more time to set up."

Ice and game reporting in general has sped up in recent years with the advent of computers. Handwriting a brawl report back in pre-computer days would take lots of time.

"I think I had the last true bench-clearing brawl, about twenty years ago, Montreal at Vancouver," remembers McCreary. "It was a full-scale brawl. I would think all officials are glad to see brawling removed. Fighting is one thing—it's part of the game—but when you have premeditated bench clearing, it doesn't make sense. I think fans are glad it's gone too; the true mentality of the fans is they want to see hard hits and exciting, skilled entertainment."

~

It would appear the officials want what's best for the game. They're fans of the game, and of the game's traditions, including their own little private set.

CHAPTER 8

Unwritten rules apply often in the behind-the-scenes officiating business, which is particularly beneficial to veteran officials, who can save some of their $84-a-day per diem at the expense of the rookies. Rookies of any type buy the meals. And linesmen and referees are rookies more than once or twice. For example, Scott Driscoll's first NHL season came in 1992: Rookie! Officials must pay the freight again, the first time they make the playoffs: Rookie! And finally, when they make it to the pinnacle, the Stanley Cup Finals, it starts all over again: Rookie! Driscoll had his twelfth season in 2004, but his first Cup Final series, so he was a rookie all over again.

Driscoll bought Scampy, Scampy's son, Ryan, Stephen Walkom, and Bill McCreary a snazzy steak dinner in Tampa that cost him about five hundred bucks. Driscoll picked up the tab for the à la carte meal, the wine, the beer, the dessert, and the after-dinner drinks without blinking an eye. Also, as standard operating procedure, he had to pick up the first pre-game meal in the series, which was another seventy or eighty bucks. This, for a guy who had originally planned to be a chiropractor.

"I had kind of planned on bagging hockey, but I had officiated since I was a teenager, and gradually made the grade in the OHA, so I just kept on going," says Driscoll.

Another hockey officials' tradition, an uncontrollable one, that Driscoll is familiar with is to expect the unexpected.

He remembers getting called off the ice in Buffalo in 2000.

"My mother had had a heart attack and died," Driscoll recounts. "It was really eerie. I had driven a trainee to the game that night, down from Toronto. I'm doing the game, and I hear the PA announcer say, 'Kelly Sutherland, please go to the referees' room.' I thought something was wrong with my wife, who was pregnant at the time. Turns out it was my mom. Someone called my wife, she called a supervisor, he called the rink, Kelly got dressed, and during a line change, Kelly came on and I went off."

Another incident, this one on the ice, definitely falls under the categories of "traumatic," and without a doubt, "unexpected." Referee Terry Gregson was on hand for the worst ever on-ice medical situation, on March 22, 1989. Buffalo goalie Clint Malarchuk had his jugular vein sliced open while covering the puck. Steve Tuttle had gone tumbling past the net and got his skate up.

"I happened to be down there," Gregson recalls. "It was a scary moment—the worst injury I ever saw. We knew Clint was in trouble right away. The players got a sense, and it was a real eerie feeling. I remember the look on Clint's face, and it was worse than panic."

As blood gushed onto the ice, the players went to their benches and the officials tried to restore some calm. Fans vomited, and at least one had a heart attack. Quick medical attention and a fast trip to the hospital saved Malarchuk's life.

"Bob Hodges and Ron Asselstine were with me. It took us a while to get back to reality. Some of the players were really shaken up. It was the only time I was involved in something on the ice that was life or death."

CHAPTER 8

Scampy never had to deal with anything so traumatic during a game, but unfortunately, he and Gregson share an incredible real-life coincidence. One day after Scampy and Gregson worked their final career regular season game together, Scampy's sister-in-law was diagnosed with a brain tumor. Later that week, Gregson's brother was diagnosed with something similar.

"It's one of those things we wish we didn't have in common," Scampy says. "That's one bond we could do without."

The old saying "the more things change, the more they stay the same" definitely applies to the officials in the sport of hockey.

"The rules and rinks have changed over the years," Scampy points out, "but the camaraderie's the same, the great feeling you get going to the rink stays the same, and my love affair with the game never goes away."

Privet (Hello) Russia

If it came down to the final five minutes of a huge game, you'd want Scampy on the lines, because there's a damn good chance he'd make the right calls.
—Scotty Bowman, coach and Hall of Famer

Igor Larionov is to hockey in Russia what Wayne Gretzky and Gordie Howe are to hockey in North America. He's the preeminent hockey legend. He started his pro career there in 1978 with the Voskresensk Khimik team, and went on to star with CSKA Moscow and later with the Russian National Team. He helped his nation win the 1981 Canada Cup, two Olympic Gold Medals, and several World Championships. He centered the famous KLM line, with Sergei Makarov and Vladimir Krutov on his wings. At age twenty-nine in 1989, Larionov jumped to the NHL, where he played sixteen more seasons, tallied 644 regular season points with five different teams, and won three Stanley Cups with Detroit. He and his countrymen on the Wings were the first men to haul the Cup back to Russia for a celebration in 1997.

He didn't score with the proficiency of Gretzky or Howe, but he represented the ultimate in puck control hockey. A solid draw man and a wizard at seeing all of the ice at both ends of the ice, he retired at age forty-three following the 2003–04 season.

In December of 2004, during the NHL lockout, Larionov staged his retirement game in Moscow. It was a private party to an extent, but it also became an international hockey spectacle. "The Professor," as he was referred to by some, flew guests and players in from all over the world. Among the guests involved in his farewell game were four hand-picked officials from the NHL.

Rob Simpson: *Tell me about being honored by Igor Larionov.*

Ray "Scampy" Scapinello: That in itself was a massive honor. I was doing a game in New York last season, and I was standing between the players' benches during a commercial when Igor was on the ice ready to, you know, be on the next shift. He came up to me and said, "Ray, this is going to be my last year," and I said, "Yeah, I understand that. Where are you going to play your last game?" He said, "I'm going to play it in Moscow." I said, "Wow, that's gotta be a thrill for you," and then he said to me, "I'd really like you to be a part of it." I said, "When's that gonna be played?" and he said, "Well, in early December." I replied, "Well, I'd be honored to do it. I'm going to retire at the end of this year and I'd consider it a great honor that you asked me to do that." And he said, "Well, after the game, if you could give me your e-mail address and phone number I'll make sure I get the information to you." And that's how it all started, and I was just so honored. There are so many NHL officials and he chose me. I was really honored that I got to do it.

Rob: *Who were the other guys?*

CHAPTER 9

Scampy: The referees were Dan Marouelli and Paul Devorski, and the other linesman was Danny McCourt. How he chose the four of us I'm really not sure, but um, Igor's such a gentleman. You know, I never did ask him why he asked me or the other three guys, to be perfectly honest with you.

Rob: *I'm assuming he had a certain fondness, maybe through reputation ...*

Scampy: I hope so. You know, he's the consummate professional, that man.

Rob: *Alright, tell me about ... had you been to Moscow?*

Scampy: No, never. The guy that organized it was Igor Kuperman. He was who I was in contact with ninety percent of the time. He used to work for the Winnipeg Jets years ago and I certainly recognized the name, and as soon as I saw him in Moscow I remembered him. But Igor had arranged the flights. Igor had arranged our passports and our visas to be in Moscow for the four or five days that we were there. I mean, we had those passports and visas in four days, so they were really well connected.

Rob: *Maureen decided not to go, although wives were invited?*

Scampy: Maureen's mother was celebrating her eighty-seventh birthday, and she wanted to be on hand for it.

Rob: *You didn't take your sidekick Dan Mathieson and you also neglected to take the author of this book.*

Scampy: Ha ha ha ha ha ha ha. I was just trying to save Igor some cash! Ha ha ha ha ha ha ha ... ha ha.

Rob: *Um, what was it like when you got there?*

Scampy: Wow, well, the first person we saw at baggage claim was Igor (Larionov). We walked out of customs and immigration, went to the baggage claim area, and there was Igor ... first guy to greet us, gave us all a kiss, made sure we all got our bags, made sure we all got on the bus, and he came down with us to the Marriott in downtown Moscow, which is a five-star Marriott—place was gorgeous.

Rob: *You actually rode over with who?*

Scampy: No, who's on first.

Rob: *Ha ha, no, flew over with ... ?*

Scampy: I flew over with the other three officials and Scotty Bowman ... and Don Beasley, the player agent. The flight was eleven-and-a-half hours over, and obviously I never had the opportunity ... I'd been on the ice for thirty-three years but there's really been no situation where I sat down and chatted with Scotty Bowman. But, we chatted a lot, all four of us with Scotty, and he just told some wonderful stories. Man, I was hoping the flight would last another three or four hours just to listen to more stories he told.

Rob: *Bigger yapper than you expected?*

Scampy: He was very pleasant. At one point I said to him, "Are you really Scotty Bowman?" He says, "C'mon Ray, I'm off the ice now, ha ha ha ha."

Rob: *And he was actually kind enough—thought enough of you—to write the foreword for the book.*

Scampy: Yeah, I was honored by that. I was actually a little intimidated to ask him. I'm honored that he would do that for me.

CHAPTER 9

Rob: *Alright, so you get there, Igor picks you up, and then what happens?*

Scampy: Well, we took a bus downtown to the Marriott. We got all registered in there, and … it was later in the day, so that evening, Igor had arranged a little dinner for all of us, right across the street from the Marriott at the … a little place I can't remember the name of it. We had dinner there and his wine was there, Triple Overtime, and we had a wonderful meal that evening, and everybody went to bed later that evening after the dinner.

Rob: *Is that the Saturday or the Sunday?*

Scampy: That was on theeeeeeeeeee … Saturday—that's when we arrived in Moscow.

Rob: (looking at itinerary) *The Music Club News Pub.*

Scampy: There you go. That's where we were.

Rob: *Some cool names there. The next day you ate at the Literacy Restaurant. That's only for people who can read.*

Scampy: That place was unbelievable. That place, it looked like an old library to be honest with you, and they had the servers all in tuxedos, and up in the balcony there were three young ladies dressed in evening gowns playing a harp and violins and they just played throughout the whole meal. And again the meal was, oh jeez, we had steak and it was just unbelievable, and all kinds of smoked fish. I guess they like their smoked fish in Moscow. And vodka, you know, I'm not … at best I drink a couple beers. I'm not a hard liquor drinker by any stretch of the imagination, but I did toast Igor with some vodka. It was high octane, trust me. Ha ha. But the meal was incredible, and Igor, he just went from person to person and he toasted them and shook their hand, and hugs and kisses. I can't say enough about this guy.

Rob: *Right. He is, I'm not sure people realize—he's kind of getting older—but for the [understanding of the] younger folks, he was considered the Gretzky of Russia.*

Scampy: Oh, no question. He is, he's as prominent as Wayne Gretzky is in North America. Igor is the same in Europe. He's just, he's a real gentleman. He's just a perfect gentleman.

Rob: *I mean, who else, if you're not at that level, how could you possibly fly thirty-plus players over and officials over to have your own farewell game, obviously that's big …*

Scampy: Exactly. The game was sold out. After the game was over—and we're talking about an all-star game here—and after the game was over, the media on the ice was unbelievable. It was like … I've done several Stanley Cup Finals and there was as many media on that ice surface as any Stanley Cup Final I ever participated in.

Rob: *Let's run through the rosters here.*

Scampy: Oh. Impressive, eh?

Rob: *Team Russia. Let's see, did he have some old-timers from the Red Army days?*

Scampy: Krutov, and who played for um, hold on here. Where the hell is he here … Fetisov!

Rob: *Oh yeah.*

Scampy: Fetisov. He's the minister of sports over in Europe. I mean, this guy, he runs the show over there.

Rob: *Let's see. What about NHLers? Sergei Gonchar, Oleg*

Tverdovsky, Pavel Bure, Andrei Nikolishin, Slava Kozlov, Sergei Samsonov, Ilya Kovalchuk—wow, he had the young-sters over there—Sergei Brylin, Valeri Bure, Viktor Kozlov, Pavel Datsyuk, Valeri Kamensky, Alexei Zhamnov, Sergei Fedorov, Alexei Morozov ...

Scampy: Impressive, eh?

Rob: *Now Team World.*

Scampy: Brett didn't play, though.

Rob: *Brett [Hull] didn't play?*

Scampy: No.

Rob: *Brodeur, Osgood, Fischer, Ward, Lidstrom, Ozolinsh, Dandenault, Chelios, Duchesne, Shanahan, Maltby, Robitaille, Jay Pandolfo, Lapointe, Gomez, McCarty, Elias, Draper, Zetterberg, Whitney, and Holmstrom, and [Igor] flew them all over.*

Scampy: Yep, absolutely. Every one of them. Some of them were already over there, playing in that world tour, but, you know, they would have been flown over, but some were already in the area, like ah, Martin Brodeur for sure, and who was over there, I really can't tell you ... ah, Luc Robitaille, he was playing over there.

Rob: *Not on this list, but a guy who showed up, was Steve Yzerman.*

Scampy: Exactly. Stevie Y. played. And he played the last period for Team Russia ... scored a goal too, ha ha ha.

Rob: *And the old Detroit coaching setup, Scotty Bowman, Dave Lewis, and Barry Smith. Talk about the tour they gave you of Red Square and the Kremlin.*

Scampy: That was so impressive. It was a private tour as a matter of fact, and two buses went. We waited outside until

Igor showed up, and then we walked in there like we owned the place. And then we had a private tour of the Imperial Palace. Oh man, the opulence in there was just incredible—the murals on the wall, the gold, marble floors—it was so impressive. Prior to going in, actually after we left, we watched the changing of the guard. That was really impressive, the spit-and-polish. I don't know if you ever witnessed it at the Tomb of the Unknown Soldier in Washington, but it was very similar, and the spit-and-polish, it was impressive. Red Square, Lenin's Tomb, it was very impressive.

Rob: *That night you went to the Bolshoi, saw the Nutcracker Ballet, which is right up your alley.*

Scampy: It was, ha ha ha. The Bolshoi Ballet was only about two blocks from the Marriott where we stayed, and we walked down. It's a real gloomy building on the exterior but on the inside it was very impressive and I ended up sitting in the third row! Yeah, I was very impressed. I sat beside, ah, Danny McCourt and his wife, and the Canali rep ... tried to mooch a couple of suits, but that didn't work out at all.

Rob: *My one experience with the ballet: I got tired of clapping.*

Scampy: Yeah, I know. As a matter of fact, when it was over, you know, we stood up and applauded, gave 'em a standing ovation, and they closed the curtain. Then the prima ballerina came out again along with the male lead, we applauded again, the curtain closed. Now we're filing out, and they kept coming out, ha ha, they kept coming. I wondered when we were going to put an end to this.

Rob: *But you also ... every time they finish a segment, you clap. They don't do very long segments. It's like, they'll dance around for four or five minutes and you're clapping.*

Scampy: You went to the Bolshoi?

Rob: *Yeah. In Hawaii. A touring deal.*

Scampy: Wow. Yeah, this was impressive.

Rob: *I mean, you're clapping your butt off all night.*

Scampy: Yeah, heavy on the applause. Ha ha ha ha ha ha ha ha ha ha. Heavy on the applause. It was a unique experience.

Rob: *They're athletes.*

Scampy: Oh!

Rob: *To an extent, I mean, in some way, shape, or form.*

Scampy: I've done those things on the ice, but never on purpose, spun around like that, ha ha ha ha ha.

Rob: *No majors or minors handed out.*

Scampy: It was impressive. I sat and wisecracked through the whole thing probably, but they are extremely talented and it was a thrill to say I went to the Bolshoi Ballet. Can't spell it mind you, but I could go there.

Rob: *B-o-l-s-h-o-i, at the Bolshoi Theatre. Then you went to the jazz music party at the Metropol.*

Scampy: That was a hotel. They had, you know, as it says on the itinerary there, there was all kinds of entertainment ... it was just entertainment, jazz musicians, again excellent. The entertainment throughout the entire time we were there was mind-boggling. I'm getting ahead of myself, but the last night we were there, after the farewell party at the Napoleon Hall—again an unbelievable meal—again, they had entertainment from the time we started, local entertainers. We're talking cream of the crop. They just went on one after the other for the whole dinner. Three hours of entertainment, and very impressive singers and dancers. Igor's daughters sang, who are singers, two young ladies, excellent singers, and Chris Rock was there; he was traveling with Cheli', Chelios ...

Rob: *Kid Rock?*

Scampy: Kid Rock. Who'd I say?

Rob: *Chris Rock's the black comedian ...*

Scampy: Ha ha ha ha ha ha ha ha ha ... he was there, too. Ha ha ha ha.

Rob: *No he wasn't.*

Scampy: Kid Rock, yeah. He was traveling with Darren McCarty. Spent most of his time with Darren McCarty and, uh, Cheli'. Chelios. And he entertained. Almost every night there was entertainment; Kid Rock belted out a couple tunes. He's a really nice guy, very pleasant guy. I obviously didn't have any opportunity to meet him before that, but met him there and [he was] very pleasant.

Rob: *Right. He's a Detroiter.*

Scampy: Oh, absolutely.

Rob: *Guys from Detroit are usually smarter than most of the general public.*

Scampy: There you go, ha ha ha.

Rob: *And then you said goodbye?*

Scampy: Yep, the next day, a matter a fact. Scotty [Bowman] ... we weren't sure when we had to go to the airport. Scotty was all over that. He had our driver set up, he made arrangements with me and the other officials as to what time we were meeting in the lobby, and we were there right on time. The bus was out front, the little van we took, and we went to the airport. And Scotty had made arrangements for the kid who was looking after us, for what time we'd be at the airport, and the kid was there, and he walked us to the ticket counter, and he walked us to customs and immigration. The flight was … Aeroflot flights were beautiful, big. They weren't 747s, but big DC-10s or 767s. We all sat in business class and were treated extremely well. And the funny thing was, as a matter of fact, when we landed in Toronto, that was the last night of the program, the one you were going to be part of, the final cu' … the umm …

Rob: *Last night of Making the Cut.*

Scampy: Last night of *Making the Cut*, and Scotty had to be there, and they picked him up. He went flying through customs and immigration, and I yelled, "Hey Scotty, we're with you," but he didn't wait for us. They just carted him right through like he owned the airport, into a limousine, waiting limousine, and out to the … I think he was there just in time for his introduction.

Rob: *Yeah, I saw the show. He came walking in. That's cool. That's kind of nice, him arranging stuff. Who'd have ever thunk it, after all those years: Scotty Bowman, your personal assistant.*

Scampy: Yeah, he was good. He was wonderful. He was, you know, I can't say enough about Scotty Bowman, I can't say enough about Igor Larionov. Ah, I told Igor, at one of the many dinners, I sat down and told him, "You know, Igor, I'm honored to be part of this and I consider it one of the highlights of my career." Which it is. We were treated like royalty, the meals were unbelievable, we were treated well. You know something? It is a highlight of my career.

Rob: *Ray, great story. Congratulations.*

Scampy: Oh!

Rob: *The perfect lead-in to chapter ten.*

Scampy: Which is … ?

What's Left Behind and Lies Ahead

*Ray Scapinello set the bar by which future linesmen
will be judged.*
—Mike Murphy, NHL Vice President of
Hockey Operations

At some point in the not-so-distant future, Ray Scapinello will be inducted into the Hockey Hall of Fame. Based on longevity alone, he's a lock. He's dressed for more NHL games than any other human in history, and there's a very good chance his records will never be broken.

Back when Scampy started, it wasn't unusual for guys to work ninety or a hundred games a season. They'd go from one game to another, to another, night after night. Now, officials are contracted for seventy games a season, and for financial reasons—overtime pay such as it is—the League doesn't really want guys to go over that number.

Based on the math, it would take a linesman approximately thirty-five seasons plus another fifty games to get to Scampy's 2,500. And, officials generally don't get hired as young as they did before.

"I can't see anyone working from age twenty-five to age sixty [as an official]," Scampy points out.

Throw in potential injuries, work stoppages, off-ice emergencies, and family matters, and you're looking at one very tall order.

In thirty-three years Scampy never missed a regular season assignment. As for the playoffs, Ray worked a record 426 games. He sat out once on purpose (see chapter five). Do these numbers alone make Ray Scapinello "the greatest" linesman to ever work? Most fans believe Wayne Gretzky is the greatest player of all time, particularly based on his statistics, but the numbers don't address all of the issues. Head to head, Gordie Howe would have kicked the crap out of Gretzky, and never before, and maybe never again, will the League's leading scorer also be the NHL's most intimidating figure. Some would argue numbers don't tell the whole story, or explain a difference in eras.

For many or most fans, "the game's greatest linesman" might not mean a whole lot, but for the sake of discussion, most realize Scampy's career performance transcends his numbers.

The greatest honor an official can earn is a trip to the Stanley Cup Finals. As pointed out, an official starts by getting to the playoffs, merits his way ahead from round to round, and, eventually, he may be invited to work the last series. Two referees and four linesmen split the Finals. Scampy earned the Stanley Cup Finals twenty times, including in his farewell season. Playoff overtime should be too much for a fifty-seven-year-old: no line changes, no TV breaks, going hard, back and forth, for fast, long stretches. Meanwhile, Scampy continued to be able to make good calls, help control a game, and control players.

"I spent a lot of time my first two seasons with Ray," says NHL linesman Brad Kovachik, who joined the League in 1996–97. "I learned a great deal from Ray, maybe more so than anyone in hockey. On the ice, but more importantly off the ice, it's how he handles himself, treats other people. He's truly professional and sincere. It's an unbelievable honor for me to be associated with him; he's maybe the most respected official I've ever seen. The players laugh with him, but most importantly, they feel they were treated fairly. I watched the standing ovation he got during his last night in Buffalo," Kovey continues. "I enjoyed the night, but also realized we were watching the best-ever linesman doing his last ever game. Two great guys and officials [referee Gregson the other] were working their last game ever."

Baseball pitching coaches talk about "positive mental make-up." This also happens to be the most important attribute in an official, and Scampy is the poster boy for positive mental make-up.

"He's a real unique official," declares NHL VP of Operations Mike Murphy, "with his combination of conditioning, knowledge, and ability. To continue at the high level for the duration of his tenure, while working as long as he did, proves what a remarkable individual he is. Everyone appreciates his personality, good judgment, and common sense. We'd love to still have him. The future's up to him."

For Ray, his diligent work ethic led to consistency.

"I'm as nervous for Game One of the season as I am for Game Seven of the Finals," Scampy points out. "I want to do the job to the best of my ability regardless of the game. Obviously the situation doesn't affect the rules or our ability to carry them out, and if it does, you shouldn't be working."

~

Just as important as being consistent, professional, and fit, is the ability to pass on to other officials the knowledge and experience one has gained.

From the perspective of other linesmen, Scampy kind of kept to himself during the first ten or twelve years of his career while he was attempting to perfect his craft. He didn't often overtly offer advice or share comments, but after eventually settling in, he wholeheartedly became a teacher.

"I remember when I started in the National League in '79, guys would say he wouldn't help you, this and that, and he kind of kept quiet," comments Wayne Bonney, "but every time I worked with him he was a great teacher. There was nothing he wouldn't do to help me out. 'Maybe you should do it this way, maybe try this,'" Bonney says imitating Ray. "He was a professional every game he had. He had fun, but he did the job. I worked with him a hundred times and he was awesome."

"In terms of passing on advice to young officials, it's more just the experience factor, and of course [the] work ethic," Scampy reiterates.

CHAPTER 10

In 2004, Scampy began helping out Ontario Hockey Association officials at the request of former NHL ref Lance Roberts. He takes in games and camps within about a forty-mile radius of his home in Guelph. Scampy remembers his first meeting with about thirty prospective up-and-coming officials.

"I was sitting exactly where you're sitting, about thirty-five years ago," Scampy told them. "So, it comes full circle. I'm here to help you. I'm not here to criticize. If I think I can help you with something, I'll mention it to you. You can use it if you want to, or you don't have to use it."

Scampy has since started supervising in the OHL, and he is also doing some supervising in the Central Hockey League, occasionally flying down to Texas or Louisiana to help out the young officials and his buddy, the man in charge of the linesmen and refs, Wayne Bonney. It's just a little more hockey geography under the belt for a guy who's seen plenty of it.

"I went to an opening Junior-B game [in Ontario] the other night," Scampy said in September of '04. "Michael McCreary, Billy's youngest son, is a linesman. Roberts is heading up the whole area. He told us, 'These three guys are the best we have and you can judge the others by them.' They covered for one another, slid through the zones, and did a real nice job."

Legacies are common in officiating circles in all sports, and hockey is no exception. Kerry Frazer's boy Ryan is a minor league referee; Don Koharski's son Jamie is a referee and so is his younger brother Terry.

"Terry's a pretty good official, just never got a break," Scampy points out.

Potentially joining these ranks after playing college hockey, and making a run at the minor pros, is Ray's son, Ryan.

"I'm finished playing at Lake Forest in Chicago," Ryan said in January of 2005. "It's division-three. We played small colleges in Wisconsin, University of Wisconsin this and that. I'd like to give the minors a shot. The ECHL would be my first choice, but I'd go to the Central League or UHL if necessary."

"Ryan's a hard-nosed, dirty little bugger," Scampy says proudly. "Kind of like a Mike Keane, Darcy Tucker type. He was fourth on the team in scoring his junior year, and then went on to be captain. He can't move his feet like me, not as fast, but he's tough on his skates, tough to knock off, and has a heart like a lion."

"After a shot at the minors," Ryan continues, "I really do plan to throw on the zebra stripes, start in the OHA, and then work my way up just like anyone else. Why not? I've got the best teacher in the world sleeping one room over from me; plus I love hockey. I'd definitely start out as a linesman and maybe stay there. I've never really thought about being a ref."

"He can pursue whatever he'd like," Scampy points out, "just as long as he's happy and productive at what he's doing."

∿

Just the fact that Ryan can talk about becoming an official, and has the physical ability to play hockey, is a testament to his mother, Maureen, the same person Ray credits for making him one of the best officials in history. Scampy insists his career would not have been nearly as long and as successful if it hadn't been for his wife.

"With all the travel in the winter, the weird schedules, and of course the basic time and pressure demands, the right partner can mean all the difference," Ray says. Maureen is definitely the successful woman behind Ray, the successful man.

"Ryan was a severe asthmatic, so severe he'd often require hospitalization. Maureen became so in tune with asthma and its symptoms and treatments, the family pediatrician asked Maureen if he could take her meticulously detailed home medical journal to a conference he was attending," Ray boasts. With this is mind, it's understandable Ray had peace of mind regarding his son when on the road.

"I'd call and say, 'How are things going?'" Ray explains. "She'd go, 'Oh, everything's fine. Ryan had a minor bout but he's doing well.'"

In reality, Ryan would be in hospital. He'd be at the hospital for three or four days and Ray wouldn't find out about it until after he returned home. Maureen knew Ryan wasn't in grave danger, so she didn't present a dilemma or distraction for her husband working away from home.

"In twenty-five years of marriage, I never received a, phone call from Maureen saying, 'Oh my gosh, come quick,' or 'I've got a situation I can't handle,' or 'Ray, I'm really worried,'" Ray stresses. "She made a point of becoming an expert."

Ray also can't ever remember Maureen calling about finances, or any problem. It's what Ray calls "a massive burden off an official," because an official has enough extra crap to worry about.

"She also never complained when I was doing a game in Florida while she was shoveling snow in Guelph," Ray concludes.

"Ray has a remarkable sense of humor. He's a wonderful guy to live with, really enjoys life, and thankfully, he's left the practical jokes away from home for the most part," Maureen points out. "He's had a few for Ryan over the years, but obviously never malicious, and he's taught Ryan to laugh at himself. It's hard to know where Ray stopped and Ryan started; they're very much alike, although Ryan's a couple inches taller." It must be evolution, because Ray's five foot six-ish, Maureen's only five foot two, while Ryan turned out almost five foot eight.

The dedication to handle Ryan's affliction can't be overestimated.

"It was a way of life for us," Maureen points out. "He had to take medication four times a day. When he was small, in school, I would go at noon with a compressor in my car that plugged into the car lighter. He'd put on what's called a Ventolin Nebulizer mask, and each treatment took about ten minutes. He did it after school also, around the clock, plus extra treatments when he had a cold or was wheezy, or when he had hockey games. People don't realize what he went through to get where he is today."

"My mom kept everything together," Ryan points out, "kept everything under wraps, under control. She's unbelievable dealing with all that stuff. We went through a lot."

"I have an outstanding relationship with him, because [of] all of the time we spent together," Maureen adds. "We always kept him active, to help fight his asthma. He wanted to play hockey desperately, but with the mold in the dressing rooms, the cold rinks, it was a lot of extra work.

"It was alright," Ryan says. "When I was in hospital, Bob Cole and Harry Neale on *Hockey Night* used to say hello to me and tell me to feel better."

"I remember at age seven or eight, he was in hospital because of frequent wheezing," Maureen continues. "I remember him saying his goal was to play college hockey. I'm so proud of him. If he never does another thing in his life, he's made it to a place he said he'd make it. Knowing how sick he was, to reach that goal, after all of the medicines and things he had shoved down his throat, that's something."

"Maureen and Ryan are very close," Scampy confirms. "They spent so much time together and went through so much with the asthma. They're much more affectionate than I ever was. Ryan wants to be with us. He calls us from school every other day. I attribute that to Maureen as well. She comes from a very close-knit family."

Scampy has adapted to the affection. His family was all business, old-fashioned, hard work and hard knocks.

Scampy's relationship with his parents blossomed later in life, although throughout, he was much closer to them than he's willing to admit. He's the spitting image of his father, and patterned his work ethic after the old man. For the most part, Scampy is simply private about his emotions.

"The Ray that people know in the business, there's really a different side to him. He's not the control freak that he is when he goes to work," Maureen says. "He's interested in family."

"My mom taught Maureen how to cook," Scampy points out. "When your Italian mother-in-law lives across the street and she's a fantastic cook, you don't get in a competition."

"It was a great help having Ray's parents right across the street," Maureen concludes. "I'll always be very grateful. I didn't have any family here; my family was in Toronto."

"I thought my granddad was the greatest person in the whole wide world. It was great to grow up across the street from him," Ryan points out. "The pride he showed in everything ... and Grandma would do anything for you, an old-fashioned Italian lady, and a great cook."

～

But let's face it, Ryan's bona fide bonus childhood mostly stemmed from the fact Scampy officiated in the NHL. The best example came in 1986 when Scampy was just five or six years old. Scampy managed to arrange "hockey day" for everyone at Ryan's school, St. John's in Guelph. Ray asked Scotty Morrison if they could have the Stanley

Cup for the day. Morrison said yes, and Scampy turned the school gymnasium into a mini Hall of Fame. It cost two dollars to get a picture taken with the Cup, with a buck going to the school and a buck going to the Hall of Fame. The whole school prepared, all grades participated, and everything was related to hockey. The math problems were all based on calculating the speed of traveling pucks and counting hockey sticks.

"The high school kids across the parking lot didn't believe it when they heard the Cup was there," Scampy remembers. "A lot of them skipped the visit and realized later they had missed the Stanley Cup."

Maureen helped decorate the gym with some of Ray's old pictures, sticks, and memorabilia he had collected along the way. She was nervous about Scotty Morrison seeing some of the goods, worried that the boss might see the extent of what Scampy had accumulated on the job.

"Don't worry, Maureen. I know he's got them and I know how he got them," Morrison said at the time.

To this day, the kids (now grown-ups) in the neighborhood always remember hockey day back in 1986.

"How would you like to go behind Ryan Scapinello for show-and-tell?" Maureen laughs.

"I'm the luckiest of all these people," Ryan admits. "I appreciate everything he's done for me, the special perks that come with his job—like working out with Lindros during the summer. I appreciate all of this stuff. It's been fantastic. Whenever Dad asked me who my favorite player was, he'd then go and get me stuff from the guy. I had a thing for the tough guys, so I have items from Domi, Ray, and Simon, and a stick or two from Gretzky and Bourque as well.

"If I was in his situation, I'd do exactly the same thing," Ryan continues. "He was always generous. I never once in my life had to pay for equipment. I'd tug on his pant leg and say, 'Dad, I need new elbow pads.'"

As he aged, Ryan then started to enjoy travel perks, and being put "on scholarship." That's the playful term for when a group of officials on a trip cover the expenses of the sons, daughters, and/or wives of the officials. Free food, drinks, and hockey tickets for a family member equates to being "on scholarship."

"Ryan got to skate with us, and eat with us," remembers ref Stephen Walkom. "He was on full scholarship for the 2004 playoffs. Maureen came out for a bit as well. I started Ryan on scholarship and Billy Mac took him off—too many wives around [on scholarship as well] squashed it."

"During the finals in Tampa Bay last year, McCreary took me off scholarship," Ryan says with a laugh. "I think he was sick of buying me dinner."

Along the way, Ryan watched Montreal win the Cup in '93, the Rangers win it in '94, and Detroit sweep Philadelphia in '97. His favorite game, however, was his father's 2,500th and final, in Buffalo.

"The ovation, sharing that night with him, the respect he got from everyone," Ryan remembers, "that was unbelievable, and the Buffalo people were first class."

This all sounds like a pretty good testament for the "family first" mantra.

"I'm not sure that was always the case, especially early in my career," Scampy says, "but you soon realize nothing else matters but family and friends."

Scampy's friends range from eighteen to eighty years old, from thin to fat, from bald to hippie, from dumb to Rhodes Scholar.

"We're no better or worse than anyone else," Ray always says. He banters with everyone at the rink—the trainers, the equipment staff, and the fans.

"It's difficult to cover it all," says NHL ref and fellow Guelphite Bill McCreary. "We don't spend that much time together during the off-season because we spend so much time together during the season. However, we will golf; in fact, Scampy will golf anytime, anywhere, in any weather.

"My daughter Melissa had a stroke when she was four years old," McCreary continues seriously. "Scampy takes her skiing, he takes care of her, I mean, there's not much else to say."

Ryan Scapinello and Ryan McCreary played junior-B together in the OHA.

"I remember the two Ryans went to Calgary when they were in midget to play in the Midget Max tournament," Scampy says, "a big hockey tournament. The organizer invited these fourteen-year-olds from Guelph to come out and play. So, Ryan and Ryan fly out there, their first time out of their own backyard, and those big farm boys just mopped up."

"Mom, you have no idea how big these guys are," Ryan Scapinello said at the time.

"This gave Ryan a good idea of how tough it would be to ever make it pro," Scampy points out. "These kids were four to six inches taller and thirty, forty pounds heavier than our kids."

Ryan fought through the size issue as best he could, literally. The *Calgary Sun* newspaper ran a photo of young Ryan Scapinello fighting. The headline, referencing a photograph of Ray, ran something like This Father Knows Best.

"Ryan was getting in his fair share of fights," Ray states. "The paper said, would his father condone it? Sure, absolutely," Ray concludes.

∼

While Ray leaves behind his on-ice legacy, hangin' 'em up means his off-ice legacy can grow even faster. The antics and attitude will transfer from the rink to recreational retirement.

"I enjoyed Scampy in the room because of his sense of humor," says NHL referee Stephen Walkom. "He's also very active away from the rink. We'd go on a hike, go golfing; if we were out west he'd be interested in going skiing, although it's taboo for injury reasons. It kept him young in a young man's game, and by the way, he kept us young."

"I don't like sitting around," Scampy states. "As a retired old guy now, I go to bed early, and get up ridiculously early. Heck, I cut the lawn three times a week. I like to do stuff. If I'm in Europe, I don't see myself walking around a building and saying, 'Oh boy, 1600s, fantastic.' I'd rather find a golf course or go water skiing somewhere different."

CHAPTER 10

The regular water-skiing fix for Ray comes while up north during the summer. When Ray and Maureen go to their rental cottage every year, it's like a home for the wayward, à la Grand Central Station. Ray acts as "cruise director," setting up activities and planning social events, all while busting the balls of each week's particular grief taker. Week to week, the person taking the most verbal abuse seems to change.

"Dan Mathieson and his family will drop in for five days ... Dan will take abuse. Ron Foyt and his crew will come in for nine days ... Ron will take some grief. And Ryan's buddies are there all the time mixing it up," explains Scampy.

Mathieson, the thirty-five-year-old mayor of Stratford, Ontario, who is on the board of the junior hockey program there and used to officiate in the OHA, met Scampy in 1998, and quickly became one of his closest friends, his advisor, and his confidant. Dan and Scampy sit and tell stories together.

"Brad Kovachik, fellow NHL linesman, was close friends with a guy in Stratford named Dan Mathieson," Scampy starts. "At one point, I asked Kovachik if he knew anyone that had a truck that I could use. I was doing a couple games up in Montreal, wanted to take the opportunity to do some snow skiing at Mt. Tremblant with Ryan, Maureen, and our friend Jason, and I wasn't sure if I was going to fly up or drive there."

"Do you need a truck?" Kovachik asked at the time.

"Yeah, that would be great," Scampy answered.

"Well, my friend Dan Mathieson works at a dealership

in Stratford," Kovey continued. "Dano will get you a truck."

"Dan Mathieson? Who the hell is that? This guy, who doesn't know me from Adam, is going to give me a truck, for a week, to drive up to Montreal to go skiing," Scampy reacted to Kovey with disdain.

"Oh yeah, he'll do that," Kovachik answered.

"You gotta be joking," Scampy said.

"No, he will," Kovey assured.

"Yeah? Okay, well I'm going, so I could use the truck," Scampy declared.

Not only did Dan give Scampy his company demonstrator, he and another guy delivered it up to Scampy's golf club, and gave him the keys, the ownership papers, and the details on it. The group had lunch together, and a friendship was born.

At the time, the boss at Dan's dealership said, "Where's that truck going?"

"Oh, it's a test drive," Dan assured.

It was a brand new Ford Expedition, the year the model came out, and after two days the owner of the dealership wondered what was up.

"So where's that truck?" the boss asked.

"It's alright, it will be back any day," Dan guaranteed.

After five days, Dan had to stretch it. "Yeah, that truck is due back today, but I'm gonna drive it for the weekend."

"Alright, just make sure it's here Monday morning," the boss urged. "I have someone interested in it."

"I'm like, okay," Dan says looking back. "Monday

morning rolled around, and I was saying, 'Shit, I hope Scampy gets his butt back here.'"

Scampy made it back Sunday night, but the truck had a couple thousand kilometers on it. Dan drove it to work the next day.

"I want to take it for a ride," the boss said. After taking it for a short drive, he quickly returned with a question. "Who the hell put all the kilometers on this thing?"

How Mathieson explained that one remains a mystery.

"That's how the friendship started," Dan states.

"The funny thing is, not long after the incident," Scampy says, "the dealership owner, Peter, found out Dan knew Brad and I, and said, 'Hey, lemme know if those guys ever need a vehicle.' From that point on, we used to exchange hockey tickets for trucks."

On another occasion, Mathieson took the manager of the dealership down to Detroit for a game.

"The manager thinks he's gonna get deluxe seats and all the bells and whistles," Dan explains. "What he was really getting was simple entry to the building."

"When are we gonna get our tickets?" Peter asked Dan.

"Well, in a minute. Hold on, we just have to wait out here," Dan explained at the time.

Peter and Dan were standing outside the Joe Louis Arena, where the team buses and delivery trucks pulled up. Suddenly a guard appeared.

"Hey, you Dan Mathieson?" the guard asked.

"Yeah," came the response.

"Where's the other guy?" the guard wondered.

"He's right here," Dan responded, motioning to Peter.

"Okay, come with me," the guard said as he turned.

Peter thought he was getting an escort up to his A-one seats. The guard took the two men up the back stairs, walked them out onto the main concourse, and said, "Hey, Ray says to come see him after the game. See ya later."

"That's it? That's it?!" Peter exclaimed.

A similar event occurred with another friend of Dan's who owned a car dealership. Scott Rocher, another hockey fan, had helped out Ray with a few car issues.

"Hey, one of these days I'll get you a ticket to a playoff game," Scampy told Scott.

"So, around rolls Game Six of the 1999 Stanley Cup Final, Buffalo hosting Dallas," Dan starts.

"Game Six in Buffalo!" Scott exclaimed at the time. "They could win it all! Yeah, I want to be there."

"Great," said Dan.

The two headed to Buffalo. As they were waiting in the back alley, Dan said to Scott, "Well, the game starts at 7:30, we're supposed to be here at six."

"We're here in plenty of time," Scott said excitedly, waiting by the back door.

Moments later, out walked Frank Henry, Director of Security for the Sabres, whom Dan had met on a few occasions.

"Dan, how are ya? Ya got your buddy?" Henry said.

"Yeah, here he is. This is Scott," Dan said, introducing the two.

"C'mon in," guided Frank.

Henry walked them through the bowels of the arena, into the officials' room for a look, and into the press room, where Henry walked them through the buffet line.

"This is awesome. I can't believe this, plus tickets to the game," Scott said at the time. Henry then walked the two up to the restaurant that overlooked the rink.

"Okay. Here ya go," Henry declared. "Hey, give Ray about fifteen or twenty minutes after the game before you come down, because there'll be a lot of press traffic … and if I were you, I'd try to get a seat along here, at one of *these* tables," Henry finished while pointing.

"No seats! I drove all the way to Buffalo and there are no seats," Scott said after Henry left. "And I wore a tie!"

"Well, you gotta look the part," Dan concluded.

Obviously things turned out just fine, and Scott shouldn't have been complaining. The Stars won on Brett Hull's controversial goal, the place was bedlam, and Lord Stanley's Cup made its appearance.

Through Dan trying to get Scampy deals, and Scampy setting Dan up with whacky hockey trips, the two became fast friends and essentially adopted one another. At one point, Kovachik called Scampy and said, "Hey, if you're done with my friend Dan Mathieson, I'd like to speak to him if you don't mind." Mathieson also has officiating experience, starting in the OHA in 1988, thus his relationship with Kovachik.

"Safe to say, any guy who at one time officiated in the OHA had dreams of going to the NHL," Mathieson says. "I knew a lot of guys that moved up and a few that made it all the way. Some of us, like myself, just didn't have enough talent to make it to the NHL."

While Mathieson was still an official, he helped get Ryan Scapinello a tryout with Stratford's junior-B team. Scampy's son ended up billeting with the Mathiesons.

~

Another good friend of the entire family is a high school buddy of Ryan's named Paul Tavares (pronounced Tav-air-iss). He was practically adopted by the Scapinellos, especially during the summers.

"Paul's got a license plate that says 'large size,'" Scampy points out, "but he recently dropped about ninety pounds and it doesn't so much apply anymore. I've got to hand it to him—he's like the Canadian version of the Subway guy."

Scampy has also worked Paul into his hockey legacy. He never goes anywhere to speak, or accepts any type of recognition, without randomly thanking Paul Tavares.

"It's now a running joke," Scampy says. "I have to thank Paul Tavares. Everywhere I go, even at my final game, when I give a speech, or say thanks, I always say thanks to Paul Tavares. I don't have any particular reason to thank him; it's just for fun."

Scampy visited a charity golf tournament in 2003 hosted by Marty McSorley. McSorley and the other hosts decided to give Scampy a pair of really nice Muskoka chairs for his retirement.

"Ryan and his buddies had come to mooch the meal and were hanging out in the back of the banquet room," Scampy starts. "I'm hanging out back there with them, sitting in the corner. So Marty McSorley is speaking, he thanks everybody on Earth, everyone for their involvement. He goes alphabetically and skips me."

"That bugger forgot me," Scampy said at the time. But then ...

"I'd like to take a few minutes to honor a guy ... ," McSorley went on.

"Uh oh, here we go," Scampy thought.

McSorley went on about Ray Scapinello, how he's a credit to the game, and how he bailed Marty out of fights, and then he presented Ray with the chairs. Ray went up and did his thank yous.

"I'd like to thank Bill Wakefield, who owns Windemere House, and of course Marty. Marty didn't need help in any fights. He handled himself just fine," Ray smiled.

Eventually, Scampy got to the inevitable.

"And in the end, I'd really like to thank Paul Tavares," Scampy declared.

The group in the back corner lost it. Ray says if he ever gets in the Hall of Fame, he'll be thanking Paul Tavares.

～

One thing they won't be able to hang in the Hall of Fame, is Scampy's whistle. Not his metal whistle, issued by the NHL, but *his* whistle, the sound that comes from between his teeth.

Scampy's blessed with the ability to whistle extremely loudly without the use of his hands or fingers. He developed it for child rearing. If Ryan was out playing for a while up the street, Scampy would step outside and let the loud whistle rip.

"Yeah Dad," Ryan would respond.

"How ya doin'?" Ray would ask.

"Fine," his son would reply.

"Okay, good. We're eating in ten minutes," Ray would advise.

Scampy also used it when his son was on the ice, playing in a game, particularly if Scampy thought Ryan was slacking. A loud whistle from the stands equated "step it up." He'd also use it as a warning. If someone was sneaking in behind the defense or a man was wide open off a line change, Scampy would whistle to get Ryan's head on a swivel. In the early nineties, Scampy carried it over to the NHL.

"It was nothing more than a heads-up to my peers," Scampy explains. "Like, if a guy was going to shoot it down the boards, and I was going to leave my line, I would whistle, and my partner would know I was outta there."

He'd also indicate icing that way, not that the other guy was necessarily going to miss it. None of his peers ever indicated they didn't like it. One boss, Bryan Lewis, wanted him to stop. He had no real theory behind the request, possibly just the potential confusion factor since a few coaches in the NHL have been known to whistle to make line changes.

"I get whistling; they get whistling," Scampy says.

In Toronto when he gets going, a group of fans begins whistling along.

He also used it as a distraction after breaking up fights, letting his fellow linesman know he was leading a player to the box and had his back turned. Inadvertently, it also distracts the player.

Watching video of Scampy escorting Eric Cairns of the Islanders to the box, one notices Scampy whistle, and Cairns suddenly stops his protests and steps towards the bin. Cairns wasn't the intended target of the whistle, Scampy was signaling the other officials, but the side effect was apparent on the player. Cairns's body language changed as if to realize the party's over—get in the box.

Referees have been instructed to use their real whistles to break up scrums, to get in there and distract the group—"show 'em you mean business." Scampy's built-in whistle served the same effect. Scampy thinks he probably used the whistle indicator about fifty times a game.

"It came in very handy for me," Scampy says. "[Linesman] Dan McCourt can't whistle, so every once in a while he'll try it with two fingers in his mouth as a joke."

Scampy uses the whistle at home sometimes to get Maureen's attention from outside the house.

"Not a very gentlemanly way to get ahold of your wife, but sometimes it's just too handy," Scampy admits.

~

With the whistle relegated to occasional home use, Scampy now has to start thinking about what to do with himself during the hockey season.

"First of all, with retirement, there's a hell of a lot of paperwork to deal with," Scampy states. "U.S. federal tax papers, severance package papers, pension, drug and dental, all kinds of papers. It's endless."

Paperwork won't be the only thing keeping Scapinello busy. Up until his last season, Maureen always declined trips.

"You do your job. Don't worry about me," she'd say. But during his farewell campaign, Scampy insisted Maureen visit New York City. They had a ball, shopping, visiting Italian restaurants, and taking in Broadway shows. Within six months of Scampy's retirement, the two had already made a return trip. It's no doubt more trips will follow. Add snow skiing, golfing, and water skiing, and Scampy will be busy, and staying in shape.

Scampy recently started the Ray Scapinello Fund, which benefits underprivileged children in Guelph. Ray plans to visit schools in the area to find needy children who are performing well scholastically. He'll then select a child, and pay for the kid's entire college education. In September of 2005, six hundred kids played in a four-on-four road hockey tournament in Guelph, with all proceeds going to the Fund.

"I'm not going to sit still," he says, "but there are a lot of things I'm going to miss—the routine stuff: driving down to the ACC, pulling in, teasing the guy who's on the door, honking the horn to drive 'em nuts as they open the big door, and saying hey to Sam, the rink rat."

"I hope the ice was better than it was last time," Scampy would always say.

"And skating first onto the fresh ice," he continues, "it's one of the simple pleasures, one of the wonderful things in life."

$\sim$

From camp directors, to car salesmen, to cohorts, and from princes to paupers, Scampy left a positive impression on practically everyone.

"I have nothing but accolades for him," states Leon Stickle. "Scampy had a career that no one will ever match. He stayed in top-notch shape, was one of the best skaters in the League, and he was lucky not to have serious injuries. He certainly worked for everything he got, and he'll be a great supervisor if he goes in that direction."

"No matter what type of game it was, people loved to watch Scampy race down and pick up an icing puck," remembers his former boss Scotty Morrison. "There are two things that I have cherished from Ray and Maureen. When he worked the Olympics in Nagano, I got a lovely hat box with white and black stripes. Ray had worked the gold medal game, and inside the box was a puck from that game, thanking me for letting him work in the NHL. He also gave me a very nice note when he retired, reiterating his thanks for his chance to work in the League."

For his last game, the rink rats in Buffalo presented Scampy with an autographed picture of the crew and an autographed Sabres jersey with "Scapinello" on the back, along with a large numeral 1.

Even Chicago Blackhawks owner Bill Wirtz, not the most popular guy in the Windy City in recent years, or with hockey fans in general, went out of his way at an event recently to see how Ray's son was adjusting to college life in Chicago.

"He came and asked me how Ryan was doing at Lake Forest," Scampy says.

"Scampy's kind of unforgettable that way," says his friend Mathieson. "People watch Scampy—he's fast, he's climbing all over the boards, he's bald, he's short, he's lovable, yet he's all business. Hustle and work ethic brings admirers. He doesn't drop the puck—he snaps it down. He's efficient. His body language is such that says, 'I'm on it, I'm ready, I'm enthusiastic.'"

As is often the case, Mathieson's summation applies to Scampy off the ice as well, if not more so. The two are sitting together in Scampy's backyard as Mathieson finishes the complimentary description.

"Anyone will say Ray is a class act and anyone he's associated with is a class act," Mathieson starts. "He lives by the golden rule. He treats people the way you'd prefer to be treated, then he goes the extra mile, and he takes it an extra step.

"When Ryan played in Stratford," Mathieson continues, "Scampy would spend hours at the rink, talking to players, talking to parents, answering questions, helping out. He left a big impression and was a great ambassador for the NHL. The guy is a class act, honestly. I'm mud on the bottom of his shoes."

A long pause.

"That's dog doo," Scampy replies.

"No, it's true," Dan smiles.

"No, I agree with the sentiment," Scampy says, "but that's not mud on the bottom of my shoes—it's dog doo."

Index